# UNTIMELY MEDITATIONS

Formerly from Sydney, Ken Bolton has lived in Adelaide since 1982 where he is associated with the Experimental Art Foundation, among other things running their bookshop. His *Selected Poems* appeared from Penguin in 1992. He edits *Otis Rush* magazine and Little Esther books. His poetry has been anthologized and his art criticism has been published in many Australian art magazines.

other books by Ken Bolton:

*Four Poems* (Sea Cruise Books, 1977)
*Blonde & French* (Island Press, 1977)
*Christ's Entry into Brussels, or Ode to the Three Stooges* (Red Press, 1978)
*Two Sestinas* (beer rhymes with bier press, 1980)
*Talking To You* (Rigmarole, 1983)
*Blazing Shoes* (Open Dammit, 1984)
*Notes For Poems* (Shocking Looking Books, 1984)
*Two Poems* (Experimental Art Foundation, 1990)
*Sestina to the Centre of the Brain* (Little Esther, 1991)
*Selected Poems, 1975–1990* (Penguin, 1992)

and, in collaboration with John Jenkins:

*Airborne Dogs,* poems (Brunswick Hills Press, 1988)
*The Ferrara Poems* – a verse novel (Experimental Art Foundation, 1989)
*The Gutman Variations* – a study of Lacan, the aphoristic and the meditative
(Little Esther, 1993)

# Untimely
# Meditations

**Ken Bolton**

WAKEFIELD PRESS

Wakefield Press
Box 2266
Kent Town
South Australia 5071

First Published 1997

Designed and typeset by Shocking Looking Books
Cover design Wulfe Hübermann
Printed and bound by Hyde Park Press

National Library of Australia Cataloguing in publication data

Bolton, Ken, 1949–   .
Untimely meditations.

ISBN 1 86254 432 8.

I. Title.

A821.3

Promotion of this title has been assisted
by the South Australian Government
through Arts SA.

Publication of this title was assisted by the
Commonwealth Government through the Australia Council,
its arts funding and advisory body.

The author acknowledges the assistance of the Literature Board
of the Australia Council via a grant in 1992 that enabled the writing
of some of these poems.

for Cath Kenneally

Thanks to the editors of the following magazines for publication:
*Southerly* for 'Poem (live at Birdland)'
*Subway* catalogue for 'Poem For An Exhibition ("I wonder what Paul …")'
*Otis Rush, AEDON, Critical Quarterly*
& the Conference Papers of *The Space Of Poetry* for 'Untimely Meditations';
*The UTS Review* for 'Dazed'
*Sport* (NZ) for 'Paris to Pam Brown'
*Just Another Art Movement* (NZ) for 'Empty Space'
*Otis Rush* for 'August 6th'
*Experimental Art Foundation newsletter* for 'Bad Memory'


*Thanks to John Forbes for permission to quote in full his poem*
*'The History of Nostalgia' (p. 80) at the beginning of the long poem 'Dazed'.*

# poem (Live at Birdland)

        not liking
John Coltrane
is a silly idea,

but *My Favourite Things*
has always irritated me
and I wait for

it to end,
clean my desk,
move around the room

making slightly 'wrong' decisions,

because the music is
on.
It is a small room & cleaning it

is more a matter of placement
than anything else & my timing
is off.

I clean
to put myself in a better, 'prepared'
mood, organized, a square foot

or so
cleared,
on the desk I sit at,

the desk nearby
full of *piles*,
– not simply a sea –

of books, & magazines
& brightly-coloured manilla folders with work in them
& bankcard receipts & cups & letters

&
– let me see now, when I look at it –
coins, stickytape,

pens,
& pencils –
… in jars, a clothes peg

plastic & pink,
a cup,
letters,

liquid paper (2),
more jars, cassette tapes
(piles of them

under the desk),

a small
scissors,
only one person I know

says it like that –
Nola –
I say it that way because of her,

stanley knife,
stapler, a porcelain fish,
that belongs to Paul

propping up a photo of itself – I was going to draw it –
a glass dish full of paperclips, bulldog clips,

some bobby pins

of Hazel's, a picture of my grandfather
looking like a thug – as in a mug shot for the police–
it is

the badge he wore
as ID
minding the wharves during World War II.

A little metal hand
clasps the rim of the desk lamp,
small & female & with

its own diamond ring.  It is
silver & is
meant to clasp the pages of your book, as you read,

to keep it open.  Cindy Sherman smiles
from the cover of a magazine.  Chris wrote recently
that one of the bushwalks near where he trains –

for rock climbing – is called that,
'Cindy Sherman'.
Or 'Cindy Sherman Walk'.  The books are Kenneth Koch,

Basil Bunting, *Meanjin*,
the dictionary,
Anna & Lyssiotis, Liz Grosz,

& upstairs on the
bed – the loft where I sleep – Ted Berrigan,
who has provided

many of the rewards for
reading poetry
in my life.  I forgive him

the bad poems in it
because the good ones are there
& they *do it, again! every time.*  (It is posthumous –

a last, very casual, book
*A Certain Slant of Sunlight*.)
I feel great, & go out

– for a brief hour of the night,
& return  – to be here.
There is notice of *further* books

too, to come, John
Forbes' *Thin Ice*, Pam Brown's *This World,*
*This Place.*  I do the cover for one,

I offer
to do the cover
for the other.  Note paper

– offcuts
actually – from Mark Thomson, a letter from John.
*Yes,*

I push my chair back.  It scrapes angrily
across the floor,
some imaginary floor, (nothing

scrapes here,
or slides easily,
the matting is too worn.)  Yes,

*for* **this** *I fight*
(drawing gun).  It is a rich & varied life.
Felix

at the
pub tonight,
some beautiful women, drinks

with Dave
&
Mark,

Hazel will come round!

I go up
& look again at Ted Berrigan's
poems.  Adelaide's lovely weather

making me tired.  The ladder to the loft,

as close as I will come
to *The Cindy Sherman Walk*
& lie down, looking out & down.

'Down' to the window,
& 'out' to the street outside
where I look pretty down & out too – to anyone

who looks up at me –
reading, smoking, drinking tea –
tho they never do.

# poem ('I wonder what Paul will put in this')

*for a catalogue essay*

I wonder what Paul
                          will put in this
he is in a sense
                          direct
                                    & where 'X' is
baroque
             about large & obvious meanings
Paul is economical
                          with what is to him
personally interesting, tho not person*al*


He affects the impersonal style of dressing
that is our romanticising of the 60s


the suavity
                          of the understated, the white
shirt,
             the plain suit
                                    that says 'modern world'
the heroism of anonymity,  the
                                              harshness
of the dry martini
                          – everybody drinks, right?
tho Paul maybe doesn't,  clever of him


Linda
             structures a whole world of meaning
a catscradle of meaning


7

                    & I *know* what
she is doing – in the sense
                         that she told me of it
and I reacted to its most mechanical reading
                                              I
had not seen the work
                    & she reacted to that
& now I will see it
                         it will not have suffered any
baleful effects
                    from my remarks, & I will not have
improved it
                    As she knows what she is doing.
                                                   Super
fluity
          be with me now!  & if you need not defend –
because I 'mean' nothing –
                              render me invisible & safe from
gratuitous attack
                         (not Linda's, who would defend me
but the crowds  that gather  & knock about
                                                   these places
art galleries, & places like the Exeter   I want to live
in Greece
               where insults are in another language, to which
I'm deaf, as this extra drink will render me, mild &
unprotected
                    but calm in my misunderstanding
                                                       watching
everyone move around me, *divided*
by what Jyanni does.
                    I will be on the side

of those who like it I know from experience, those
at any rate able to say so
                                    For how could you
not be interested?
                            Certain nuts resist this interest
– which they feel
                                but disapprove of – & would blame her
for interesting them
                            which is neurotic?  Well, am
I not neurotic?
                        – not relevantly in this case.
                                                        (It
will be installation, I guess
                                How propositional,
                                                        &
stimulating
                        in the sense where it exists without inverted
commas – or sarcasm
                            to which I'm not prone, critically,
that is, in my gallery mode
                                or prone, even, much,
to irony
            tho I am ironic & sarcastic enough
when joking
                but making sense is hard enough
                                                    & difficult
so I leave it out – tho joking  *is* making sense
                                                *par* excellence
ha  ha
            & so Jyanni's work will be full of it (them) sarcasm,
& irony, & I will like it.
                            I do not know Helen James


9

nor what she will show

                               She said something once

without inverted commas

                              that I could hardly credit

tho I do not really know if I heard it, as I was under

the table practically

                       by that time,  under it

                                     literally,

I think

            doing nothing but prove  the just equivalence of that phrase

with its metaphorical meaning

                         I hope nothing in the show

is as complicated as this is, in being obvious – Artist X, help me!


I admired her once

                    for lying down at an art talk

in a nightclub

               tho she was listening

                             as I have always

admired her bearing

                  Trevor's bearing I like, too

tho his beard strikes me often – let's be frank, *always* –

as a kind of inflection

                   it doesn't hide his face

                              which is friendly

& operates like irony – the *beard* does! –the face is direct

                                & the beard

is like a joke about it.   I suspect

               it goes with the job

                          maturity

                            complexity

sophistication,  order.

Taste.
Tho heaven knows the Department
is not *known* for that.
I wonder what *he* will put in it?


I show this to Jyanni

who says
*It's great, but you've left out Jim!* Jim Moss!
I forgot.
Jim, Jim!
what will you put in?

# poem

*– for Martin Munz*

Walking down from the *Star*
*Grocery* from the far side
of Morphett Street I saw

the lion on top of the Lion Building
The first time I have
noticed it, in quite a while.

Its scale is increasingly
and loveably inappropriate
to North Terrace, as it modernizes

and the lion seems small
earnest, and straightforward.
And the sky looks great beyond it.

            I have chocolate frogs
for Becky and Julie
– for Martin I just

casually stroll into the Park Lane
Liquor Store
and order a bottle of Strega

– no, Martin is in Sydney …

and that is a joke …
a famous poem
by a favourite poet

has something like that sequence –
gifts bought for people and the stroll
for Strega scotch.  My life

is miles from that – I wear
a battered leather jacket that
if I thought about I'd be embarrassed

– when could *I*
last afford scotch for someone,
or go to a dinner laden with presents?

on the other hand – I *am* a poet.

Different stars shine down on me.   I am on

the other side of the world.

Today I talked to Yvonne Rainer,
a New York artist.  I said, Hullo,
I liked your film.  And then I asked her

about the dedication to Ronald Bladen
– 'in memoriam' – I didn't know
that he was dead.  She asked –

and I said I knew just the few
well known works
and had for years.  She said

he was a painter originally, romantic,
expressionist.
There was going to be a retrospective.

I held Bladen's work in only
an affectionate regard.  I think I had
originally thought not much of it

– but the most usual photo of one,
*The Big X* (his sculpture) I had liked
and had liked to do drawings of,

sending it up, but liking it really.

At the far end of the photo
beyond the enormous X that filled
the two storey gallery, which had

classical pillars around it,
was a 19th century Roman sculpture –
Diana, say – some modest naked

nymph or woman, such a
strange contrast to the big minimal
sculpture.  I used to like doing the

drawing, to bring out this contrast.
Once I put also two people in it
small, obviously walking and talking,

oblivious, to the sculpture and the statue.
Did I? or were they
always in the photo?

I write my first fan letter –
to a favourite poet in America. I had
intended to for years. I had intended to write

to others:
Joe Turner …
This week

I have been confused, and
acting strangely, my heart
in panic at its foolishness.

*This* –
is a day for decisions. I orientate myself
between   a Frank O'Hara poem   and the sculpture,

and this new information
about Ronald Bladen, and the little lion
on the 'Lion' *building*

– in my leather jacket,
that looks, now that I recall it, like one
James Schuyler wears

in an early photograph
and that looks very 'unlike'
him

– the bomber jacket
– on such a poet – as unlikely as it
looks on me – but then, I am

hardly *here* I guess.  I
know the lion is doomed, more or less,
but I will likely be gone before it.  Is that

true?  Well, the *thought* is to the point.
It is the Canutish aspect to the lion I love –
standing dark and silhouetted,

against the brilliant clouded sunsets
that seem like history

## HOT NIGHT – JANUARY – AT THE EXPERIMENTAL ART FOUNDATION

**a consideration of poetry, some reflections on nature, the many masks of the human soul, business as usual, some final wishes, and 'The cheque is in the mail.'**

I have a serious tone of voice which

once adopted I am not even

interested in –

there is nothing it will say

that I care to hear

– though it

can say things

with which I *agree*.

But that is politics! & I fall asleep,

or run a mile,  depending.

So I have *my* vote – who cares?

This *is*

that tone of voice.

Oh dear!

Well,

while I'm at it:  <u>sometimes</u>

<u>I think English Poetry</u>

<u>has *really* dropped its bundle</u>

                              – James Fenton

& the verse & opinions in the establishment

                      English reviews.

I ride my bike

           instead up the hill to North Adelaide

– this is something

             no English poet can do –

                      hardly puffing

expounding to myself like Vlaminck

                on my greatness.

                         Well,

'no' really

       – taking in

            the glory of the night – networks of

sprinklers on,

          drenching the parklands of the town

                     after a day of

42 or 3

       – white ghostly sheets of spray in the moonlight,

                   *mist*,

                      &

their cool temperate noise,

           drifting temperately.

                                        I decide

I will stop by this park on the way back

                              when I have picked up the mail

for the EAF

                    in whose gallery I slept tonight, briefly

                                        – cooler than the room *I*

room in –

            on a table,

                        in the very

                                    centre of the gallery

                                        – like a victim or

statistic,

            or like a 'patient'

                        – *of course* –

                                        etherized

                                        upon the table –

*not* etherized, not whacked, not twisto –

                                    felled, temporarily, by a

small amount of dinner wine –

                                    minutes later

                                        woken by the flickering

of the sign

            that says 'EXIT', its persistent green

                                        catching my eye  &

despairing

        (*me* – the light I think knows nothing –

              though it has

'seen' a lot

       – some terrible art, & some good,

          & the crazed gnashing

(of teeth),

     hysteric behaviour it has seen,

         well meant co-operative

          generosity,

            despair

& boredom,

     & humour …

       … This is an *experimental* art venue –

where I unpack

    for example the artworks

       & give them their hang

– an artworld phrase or usage – 'hang'

       as a noun –

         & pull

most of the faces of Messerschmitt, the mad German sculptor,

         &

*then* some:  Buster Fiddess

      – I show here my age –

  Sylvester

                                                            Stallone

is that 'better'?          Jean Paul Sartre

                                        or *someone* sad  &  'all alone'

– a maiden on a rock –chained there – in a picture by Gustave Moreau,

with a demeanour (mine)

                        that ranges (quickly) between that of Daffy Duck

… and that maiden's!

Christ she is despondent.          The light could be said to have seen all that.

But only in a

                manner of speaking, and I get up

                                                after just a few minutes,

of that light glowing there

                        – almost blocked out by my shoulder,

tho not quite – no matter *how* I lay.)


            EXIT.



                                I have a huge pile of mail,

all to myself, at the *Terrace Coffee Shop* –

                                lovers, & couples at other

tables have each other

                & coffee & biscuits, a kid or two – but I commune

                                                        with a

whole world –

        a book catalogue from London,

                a postcard, in German or

Dutch,

    from some similarly-minded group

             in Europe, saying, in its way,

something about their new, important artist.  It is a way,

                unfortunately,

we hardly understand – & eventually

           someone will throw it in a basket,

with other rubbish,

      leaving our minds that much less edified,

              less puzzled,

less troubled

     – this is, after all, the *brief* of modernism, of the avant garde,

of the post modern – you can see

        now, the need for all those faces –

                Fiddess,

Stallone, J. Paul Sartre,

    … maybe

        T. S. Eliot's – would that prove handy?

or is he

   in fact *too risible?*

      too *easily* risible

                                        – too 'cheaply' so?

Alright then – there are other faces:

                        they all seem either –  similarly –

'too obvious',

            or, otherwise,

                  'obscure'.

                              But that is my point –

I pull all those!

                  and I can do T. S. Eliot – here!



                  (pulls face).


The cheque is in the mail


                  – that is the important thing –

                              & the reason

I am here   (in a number of senses).   It is the reason Julie,

                        the administrator,

asked me

            ('Maybe check the mail?')   in the first place

                        – so she can bank it if it comes.

I have, now, consequently, the pleased face – of

                              Gunther   (!)

                                    was he

the tall one? – in *Car 54* ?

                                 or *anyone* who looks pleased – I was

going to say Gus the Cow, but

                        who *is* that figure?  Well, it is not

*my* cheque,

              and the pleased expression

                          can only have lasted briefly

(*I* would like to think

                 – at any rate if it looked absurd).

                                 People do

see me, & say There goes that jerk, or What an

                          odd looking figure,

or even That's Ken Bolton  – sitting over there

                      – I wonder what *he's* doing.

On this night, I like to think,

                they said Ooh, what an interesting looking

man,

     what an awful lot of letters!

                  Who knows

                          what expressions

we wear – at any given moment?    I didn't look like

                       Messerschmitt

this night, not at the coffee table,

                 but something calmer, & not

a cow.

       On the way back I did stop at that park, & watched the water

                     being sprayed

& found a spot

          where water-cooled air,

                 & occasional mist,

                    would drift over me,

'occasionally' –

        & there I may have looked

                 like a relieved or

completely unaware & instinctual

          lemur,

             poised mindless in a tree.  It

took me way out of myself

        for a second.    43 degrees,  & the night but

                slowly cooling.

For a while I *may* have looked pretty out of it.

             Calm.

                I had been reading

some pretty terrific poetry

       over dinner

           and now once again my mind is

calm –

     calm  independently of air conditioning.  (Although calm,

I guess, because of something pretty similar!) – The ride down the hill
was terrific – though I was nearly run over.

By a madman.

I might
have become the *patien*t, or body

or statistic

(I was going to say
'integer'

for a second,

but I no longer know what that means –
number?

perhaps I *could* have used it?)

that I earlier in the night
prefigured.

Phew!  Luckily life is not like that.  Though there is
always some type ready at any big event to 'dignify' it

with *irony*,
& that perspective

– a voice like Clive James'  or somebody's.  Imagine –
but when you're dead you're dead & I'd as soon not have that sort of thing
heaped on me

– or not by any well-wishers.  This seems

a good

opportunity

        – surprising & unexpected – to say, I don't want any priests,
or anybody playing my supposed favourite piece of music.

                               When I die.
On the other hand, *Friends!*

            do what you like.

                 I pedalled back to the E.A.F.
through the velvet night,

          the moon no longer quite full

                  & technically,
therefore, gibbous

        – & looking pretty bright,

             as do the stars,
let myself

      in,

        took off a lot of clothes, cooled my feet
on the concrete floor,

       & after a while

          began a letter to Pam Brown,
poet,   my body cooling off,

        an expression on my face somewhere between
Art-Carney's-in-concentration

        or Chardin's child   building his
house of cards

(– concentration –)

– at any rate *not* Messerschmitt's –

pleased that I can ring Julie tomorrow

& say –

'The cheque is in the mail,'      like *an Australian businessman*,

two phrases, these last, *I love.*

# Habits of Mind

'Aint it great to be great!' – Ron Padgett

God that littoral
looks corrosive

is that a baby
or a shirt factory?

Hard to tell
in this weather

I'll be a dag
for you, baby

'Scribble scribble
scribble, eh Mr Twombly?'

(Professor Donald Brook meets
Cy Twombly.)

Bird bird bird,
bird is the word.

– Gertrude Stein.  (Laurie Duggan)
Hullo Laurie!  It is the 27th

day of November!
Did you know that?

Who knows that
in this weather?  I don't.

And you don't too.  You don't
neither, to be precise.

If you dig my meaning.
If you dig my meaning
could you put it over there?

Ah! there! where the grass
grows greener!  Or is that

a trick of the light?  which once,
we all know, stood, often,

for 'Him'.  I don't.
I stand for no one.

I sit here but!

Nutty,
sure

– but here!

# Lecture: Untimely Meditations
## (Tentative Title)

*'a stroke of undeserved luck*
*has kept the mental composition of some individuals*
*not quite adjusted to the prevailing norms.'*
Theodor Adorno, <u>Negative Dialectics</u>

*'Time is marching'*
John Lee Hooker, old song.

*'Thanks for the sour persimmons, cousin!'*
old saying

# 'Lecture'

## (Part one)

> Looking back,
> on my recent past,
>
> on my present –
> that is continuous
>
> and heads, on my right,
> if the left is the past,
>
> into the future –
>
> with none of the aplomb
> if that is the word,
>
> with none of the confidence
> of Samuel Johnson,
>
> with none of the *elan* of Frank O'Hara,
> with only a guilty and apprehensive grin
>
> because in part
> I belong to that school that says
>
> if you see a leg pull it

I begin this tour of my attitudes
and my attitudes

to the attitudes of others –
the Big Issues as they affected me,

or, even,
as they failed to get my notice,

got my notice belatedly, got
only *my* notice

and as I reacted to them
and to the reactions of others.

And some weren't all that big
but anyway …

   Viz –
**modernism, the Australian landscape,
our identity, post modernism, various**

poetic movements –
and I do it …

to be interesting,
efficacious and liked –

though to be liked
one must be slightly scandalous

and a little charming  (Can I do it?)
And because I was asked.

And I hear somebody remark

What's so important
about YOUR attitudes?

somebody who hoped I would not just
state my own

but take this opportunity
to be an expert

responsibly talking
in the voice of reason and platitude

– enunciating views
that are *not* my own?

Is that responsible?
Then talk naturally!

Though theory has taught us
there is no such thing

that even prose
is rhetoric, is untransparent –

though it is mostly prose
it has taught us that *in*.

Theory sees my point –
though I'm sure it doesn't like it.

Meaghan Morris told me once
she 'couldn't read' poetry –

because of the short lines
and all the wasted white paper:

I told her
I couldn't watch films –

unless they were on TV

with lots of ads – or video,
so one could talk

and yell with all one's friends,
and think.

It seemed an equally
small-minded answer.

Though true!

Though in my case
it is a preference,

in hers an inability.

I don't think of my ideas
as Truth, though I hope

some of them are accurate,
perspicacious, interesting –

*freighted* a little
with insight, why not?

But I 'offer' them –
regard them, report them –

as historical themselves,

as determined:
some opinions … that make

a history of opinions,

and of equivocations, lapses,
what else?

To be truthful, moments when I
'had a rest'

looked elsewhere,
grew distracted, con-

fused, came thundering back,
my mind having woken

with another opinion.
Here goes …

In the mid 70s
I became aware

of an irritating irregular din,
becoming quite insistent

– things beginning with 'I'
appropriately.

It was Les Murray

Les told us
'Where's
the beef?'

as if poems were a sandwich

and his
had dinkum verities

and content, while ours were that relativistic nonsense
you learn at unis,

not very sustaining.

This was 'The City and the Country' theme.

Les assured us the Country was
'more Australian'.

It was different.  I could see that.

So I could see how it
might be 'better'.

– Well, actually, I couldn't,
but I could see

that someone might say it.
Though, really, I wished they wouldn't.

At the same time there was around
another faction.

I hear them shout –
as though it were today  –

*'WE'RE for feeling!'*
& *'The brain's a bad guy!'*

– not quite their diction,
but their base position.

(And for a while,
women, for example,

were *only* allowed
to write of feelings

– or got accused
of

'not writing from female experience.'
The best ignored this –

and those days
are gone, except

poets who stamp their feet,
get cranky, report on

the 'dark side',

seem always to feel
– not just truculent –

but more authentic.

I can't see it.
Did I say 'Diction'?

The New Romantics
were for Belief

*and* Feeling.

They believed in Myth
and wrote of myths they didn't believe in.

Or am I giving them too much credit?

I see myself,
a New Romantic –

       'foot in the stirrups I mount
       the heavily gilded saddle –

of the white horse –

the steaming white horse –
of my imagination

– *and* set forth –
the characteristic

pose
of the New Romantic.

Characteristically
I set forth,

in the middle of my life,
lost in a dark wood,

at my kitchen table –

where I might as well be playing
*Dungeons & Dragons*

for all the good
I will do anybody –

when the Angel addresses me –
and I am caused

to lift my helmet's visor,
and my head,

and gape awfully –
and in admiration.

    (She is really beautiful

    – she, too, is dressed in costume –
    and I can tell she likes me

    – this is a visitation –
    and speaks

    as though to someone taller,
    and a good four feet behind me –

    and her lips move.

    Yet I seem not to understand,
    till seconds afterwards –

    It is a little like TV,
    where the subtitles arrive (late)

    and linger, pointedly –
    and she fades

    (like TV also)

    and I am plunged,
    or I *set forth*, and the woods grow darker ...)

which is like Romantic Poetry.

Which is the point!

You see, I am *like* those guys –
Shelley, and Byron

and the others, Keats
and Wordsworth

(is *he* okay?) –

I wonder if the Bottle Shop's still open –
*I'm beginning something major.*

What it turns out to be

is, the vindication
of my lack of Doubt,

and punishment for *almost* doubting,

but basically my vindication.
(Doubt is anathema to me.)'

'Doubt' for them

was inappropriate
to Poetry's 'calling':

(Lots of people have never liked it.)

better to mount
and ride one's charger

into an imagined realm –
of capitalized Abstract Nouns,

gods and goddesses,
and Angels

and phoney revelations –

about the pitfalls one's soul had met,
and denounced

in moments of duende.

Robert Adamson did this.
But he was only kidding.

But there I am,
doubting again.

Now he just goes fishing.

(Still, never know what you'll find
just gutting a fish –

scales in your hair,
blood on your hands,

the eye of the old fish
catches yours,

and you look in: *Dark Night
of the Soul* again,

a renewal of faith!

– in one's spouse, the River, the
tides of life.

It's possible.
It's inevitable, seemingly.

I must go fishing.)  And I am reminded –

as I was reminded then –
of the criticism,

given in the artist's time,
of Gustave Moreau

whose heroes all wore breastplates, and helmets –

the heroines in diaphanous silk –
to dance, or go maundering –

while Baudelaire would have
top hats, business suit and briefcase –

the *Heroism of Modern Day Life!*

(Which makes me think of Tranter.  Always does.
I guess it is his franchise.)

(It now consists of a pool, a few
hosties

– drunk, eating pills, spewing –

and a lesbian – a word John depends upon
to ginger things up – what else?  yachts,

cars, an overseas reference, the mention
of some disappointment, a wry twist

at the end – Marcus Aurelius in
shirt and shorts, somewhat suburban – as if

Mr Boswell  from *Happy Days* was actually an
alcoholic – which, as John would point out,

he *was!  is!*  How surprising.

John's idea of modernity has always been
a little like the Pop artists – an iconography

tied to a particular period, always
ten or so years ago – the sit-com soap

version of reality, of bad designer shirts
(and airhostesses – yes, I know – drinks,
the repertoire …)


While in real life
Bob drove an Alfa,

I always imagined Les Murray
on a tractor

or pushing a one-furrow plough –

or seated
(this is more likely)

like an enormous bad fairy
behind the people

in a picture by Millet, *The Gleaners* –
tormenting them with his poetry.

He used to 'intimate' –
is that too light a word – he was more Australian

(relatively)
than the rest of us

and went on a lot –
about his Celtic blood, and

a disappearing Australia.
This was his Mystic Wing of the Country Party phase

– an interest in guns, and
'the blood of men'.

Multiculturalism, but, had become

the Next Big Thing:
So he called his book *Ethnic Radio* –

but in a last ditch move

has taken God as an imaginary
friend –

imaginary, in-
visible, but none higher

and (and here again, it is
relative) He only likes him.

I ignored them –
Les and Adamson –

twin stars.

In their different ways
as tiresome as each other.

Opera Bouffe.
Though you could see then

which was likely
to become established.

One was marketable
as a kind of Truth
about the wider world.

Bob, on the other hand,
might be accepted

as truly a poet,
if not a poet of truth,

for believing things
sillier than anyone sane believed.

(Each is an embarrassment.)

Sillier than what I believe in.

Each of us perhaps
will admit to a silly belief.

Who will admit to one?
Whose job is it

to hold them, these beliefs?
Surely a poet's?

Who *is* that person, out there,
beyond the pale,
frothing and ranting – a poet?

As for Australia disappearing –
well, things have changed –

social justice
and democracy

seem reduced –

and invocations
of some real Australia
exclude

large portions
of the population,
citizens born here

or born elsewhere –
who don't care

*what* happened
on the River Kwai,

*who* the Queen is
or who was the guy

named after the biscuit
– or why.

*

At university I found,
in visual arts,

'the landscape tradition'.
(Thematically, here, I 'hop about'.)

I believe if I went back there,
they might *still* be doing it.

But it is an academic thing:
No one paints them anymore.

*Which is a great solution.*

Though its prominence –
as a debate at least –

is in its relation
to the *'idea'* of Australia, our need

to be independent culturally,

and to resist
ideas and styles that are foreign,

not produced by authentic Australians:

*We Should Paint Trees.*

– Which are not ideas,
admittedly,

but the idea *to paint them* is,

and is only one
(which is better).

In fact it is an English, Romantic idea –
or a German one.


You see, I think, the
parallel with Les.

*

The feeling / ideas debate
has its equivalents

in conflicts between
various styles of art –

Minimalism versus Expressionism for example –

and (again) in the
'theory' versus 'getting on with it' standoff that is more recent

And Relativism versus
Responsibility –

they make a nice pair.


Internationalism,
'cultural imperialism' …

and ideas 'too French',
too 'American'.


*'Cruel Theory'*
versus 'Spirituality' –

that one
has re-surfaced –
here even, in Adelaide!

*

Everything that's happened to me
has happened in Australia.

One of the good things
is the way the cook sings *Perfidia*

– whistles it – over the noise of
cups and conversation at *Al Frescos*

– where tout le monde
rabbit on – a song I heard as a child,

on the radio.
I loved it then
and I love it now,

its inflated delicious
romanticism and cummerbunds, big hats –

trellises of roses, the moon.  Clouds.
Does Les Murray know that song?

I feel sad and happy at the same time.
Is it unaustralian, that song,

because it's so moustachioed?

... the 'Cruel Theorists'
didn't feel

all that cruel or cold,

the Relativists
didn't feel irresponsible.

People (the too American,
too French) didn't feel it was
*Australian* to be dumb.


Cultural-imperialist vanguard-internationalist intellectuals
rarely seem to speak up.
Now why is that?

Yet P.P. McGuiness and Les Murray,
with the tone
of a rearguard action, dream on:

wet feminist lesbian left semioticians,
one might think,
rule the world

– or are colonizing it,
for a terrible Cloud Cuckoo Land
that threatens.


Like our landscapes
we avoid History.
Time produces it.

Laurie Duggan's *New England Ode*,
through its specificity,

provides antidote
to Murray's mythology

(The latter a poet
of State
and Nation,

and one with advertising:
false, hectoring, corrective,
silencing.)


I was sitting in Al Frescos one day
overcome with an abstract emotion

at the singing of *Perfidia*,    *

people banging cups
and yabbering, when one of them
detached themselves

came over to tell me I was
*'Cruel Theory'* and *'not Spiritual enough'*.

I don't have a Cruel Theory
in my body.
Plainly, I would have thought.

Personally I don't feel
ever
tied to these dichotomies

---

* Actually, Les does know that song: it is included on his CD of **Tunes for Gumleaf & Fireside** and is creditably well done.  Rounder Records ROW 197

but somewhere in-between
or unaware of them —
except when forced to focus.

It seemed an unspiritual
thing to do,

to approach someone
and inform them
of their unspiritual status.

Unless you belong to the Inquisition.
But I focus, in these situations —
we are picking sides,

perhaps the whole population
in Al Frescos
is finishing their coffees up

in order to divide and
properly have the
slanging match

that
even now goes on,
unorganized,

as I sit here,
un-spiritual.

I estimate
what is
the best unspiritual ploy to offer,

the unspiritual 'first move'.

I wonder what
the other unspiritual people
are saying.

Some faces look grim,
some romantic – is that
how it divides up?  The woman

who has told me this
resembles Madame Defarge
as a finger puppet –

How do I look?
I feel I look
like my sister's dog, Whiskey,

after she had pulled it by the tail –

from its breakfast,
a massive bowl of milk and *Ricebubbles*,
so she could then watch the dog

burp enormously,
a long, long belch like a bellows,

his swollen stomach
and his ribcage
going down,

as the air was expressed. *Rice-
bubbles* and milk he ate
in one long, in-taken breath,

lapping and lapping.

Like the dog in Gertrude Stein.

For a second
he would seem nonplussed
and stand –

staring straight forward.
Then the burp would begin –
to my sister's jubilation.

Just similarly *I* burp, my eyes
watering.

Sort of unspiritual,
sort of not. And stare forward.
I am on the unspiritual team.

Have I begun well?
an own-goal?
or begun decisively?

[Pauses For Drink Of Water.  Drinks it.]


In truth I never cared about these things –
or cared about them as they occurred specifically:

I worried about my own authenticity
         in relation
to the great art of elsewhere

and the past.  Ignoring or denying it
seemed not the way to go –

and anyway, I *liked* it:  the fabulous clouds
of Guardi and Tiepolo, the silky greys and whites and silvers

of the skirts in a Gainsborough – like the winter skies
of Adelaide; the beautiful surfaces in the poems

of Frank O'Hara, Ted Berrigan, and later
James Schuyler – and the work of

some of my friends – which was great
in *relation* to that.  And the client state delusion

– of connection, of place
in an unreal schemata … –

no objectivity I can attain has ever allowed me
out of that world's attraction.  If this is 'The West'

and The West is doomed,
the problem is not with its art – and the alternatives

were no less Western,

though they had less leverage – colonialist doxa (Les Murray)
and the pretence of spiritualized emotion (out of context,
as far as I could see)  (Adamson)

and in any case I did not believe them:

I was born in a city
with a cultural background that constituted me as

– that *word!*
or any rate, here I *am* –

relativist, self-doubting, glad
of whatever knowledge this threw up, though hard won

and fleeting.  Which sounds 'heroic' –
so it can't be true.
(I won it in the library, admittedly,

and hanging around – as I have done
the rest of my life – watching what other people do

& reading.)

The vectors 'placed' you – inescapably –
with all your class, and cultural,

and historical specificity.  Damning,
contingent, real  – about as liberating and breathtaking

as it was 'final'.

*Was* it interesting, breathtaking – was it
final?   Another sort of romanticism.

I sit in the same spot, at
the same table, at the same coffee shop
every day

and think the same thoughts.
That's the vectors.


\*

*(Pause.)*


I have paused so often, taken
so many of these little drinks.  (Drinks glass of water.)  And I
    realize:
I resemble, a little, my sister's dog.
I have lapped up, indiscriminately, ideas like these: the
    spectacle
as epistemes and Egos clash, *and* –
the expression theory of art  *– here I 'bring  it up'*.

Is this evidence? a symptom? the talking cure? –
a public self-denunciation and – Chinese-style – re-education?
      Is it
autobiography?

---------------------------------------------------------------------


**(Part two)**


Les Murray's new book has appeared –
interestingly, in connection with the Inquisition,
under the imprint Isabella.  In it

I think he talks
to the Natural World – 'things' and animals
talk to him (rabbits, rocks, plants, perhaps the air,

'The River', 'The Tree') and interestingly, I bet,
they tend to think as Les does,

their view squares with his.
Another kind of silent majority –

who you can bet
are not intellectuals, feminists, or ideologues.

\#

Of course a landscape squares up pretty interestingly
if you're a formalist – and I don't want to 'preclude' *anything*,
but 'the landscape tradition' surely does, is nothing but that,
        for a lot of happy people –

who find depiction of social relationship, social station,
        social interaction,
to be uncomfortably, depressingly, political – the real world –
where they want distant hills, innocent muzak,

or the counter myths of Australianness and nation.

The empty landscape, I can't help thinking, bears
some relation to strike breaking, shooting people, the police,
legislation against assembly,

impatience and disdain.

                        #

Escapism.
Well, there is an element of that
in much great art

 – an escape
to real sensory formal engagement –
Cezanne, say!

I don't think
the rich are capable of it.  (How
unfair, to say that.

And it *is* unfair – tho I saw one
the other night
at the opening

– ridiculous when they are identifiable –

appearing unwilling to be soiled
by the riff raff of the rest of us, requiring
the gallery owner's attendance

– *lonely, perhaps?* –

to reassure her
her discriminations were not as ours –
living in a fantasy world.  Well, we all do.

Different from mine.

#

**Question:**          Why worry about
National Identity and then sell the farm?
– the policy of our ruling class.

ID is only useful vis a vis other nations: as resistance
to external power and values – or else it's something
someone *else* complains against –

the New Guinea resistance fighter, the
Asian tourist industry, Aborigines.

Do the rich stand corrected?  Ever?  Does
investment?  I hope she bought some
bad art.  She looked like Carroll Baker –

dressed 'subtly' in all white.  Her bloke
the sort of bourse functionary
who might express his personality

through a sportscar.  Grey pants, striped shirt.
Maybe he wore a tasteful belt –
of, say, llama hide, or fine plaited gnu.

Do people buy
anymore to shore up, or *vote* for, the
National I.D.?

Or just to register their social distinction ('I think *this*
is cute,'  'I think *this* is funny,'  'See, *this*
is *my* sense of humour.')?  Do people

buy landscapes anymore?  Mandy Martin's
I guess – but that's the Impersonal Sublime:
'I'm a tough guy – I'm Romantic.'   'Lacerating,
                    isn't it?' the artworks say.

(What's she ever done, to me
[aside from the paintings] ?)


National unity of a 'higher kind' is promoted
against sectional interests (except those of Wealth,
which are identified with Nation)

and the important sorts of identity –
class, gender, locale, individual –
and the contest of values, are all to be precluded –

by Authoritarian Admonishment
that says Landscape = Nation = Patriotism and that's
sacred.

Does Arvi Parbo ever have to demonstrate his patriotism?
I just wondered.

… Is Arvi Parbo
a great guy?  Is the art-collecting
        woman?
I don't know.


                              #


*post / modernism*

about which I am
'happy to be swayed'
etc

and have no heavy opinion, insight,
or contribution to make

to the debate about the exact nature
of Post Modernism

or its consequences


In writing, the divide between what my friends and I were doing
and the others

was that they – the others – wrote of Belief
and as Celebration

or maybe despairingly
of a *loss* of faith

– which we bore with
equanimity.  Our

skepticism and relativist's buoyancy
I think were deemed modish

(or modern): They spoke
for Tradition

We could see how *we*
related –

to mostly US models in my case –
Williams, Johns, Rauschenberg, O'Hara

Berrigan and Minimalism, Robbe-Grillet –
in favour of intelligence more than touchstones

as if by touching them they might reactivate,
make, the old world live again

Tho what world?
Larkin's? that of Yeats?

(of Donald Brook & Noel Sheridan?)
or Geoffrey Hill's?

They seemed a kind of prayer
and a prayer is the dumbest thing to do

but out of touch – On the other hand, acting in
the real world,

of grants and publication, they must have been ruthless:
Murray's protestations of his innocent good faith –

guileless and plucky leader of
the Christian minority true blue genuine faction –

are hard to believe
Though meant, admittedly, for the *non*-literary world's

consumption.
A professional face

to the world
and the exercise of power among the family.


It seems to me our poetry deals
with a world

of incommensurable  (yike!)

and interestingly unsettling developments
that their poetry merely resisted –

a projection, or shadow,
of the past.

Well, maybe we are equally
an epiphenomenon, registering

what they resist,
and you can easily be interesting in

either way.
Why don't I see them as interesting?

I liked Pessoa, for instance, or
'in principle',

I liked, well, lots of
change-mourning postures

I was not unprepared to be
amused – or moved even, maybe –
…


                    #


What tiring opinions!

I like thinking
about the opinions of others –

*and then (!)*
*I have almost an opinion myself –*

but not quite, or only briefly,

& there is no poetry in it – or there is,
but it is in it accidentally.

Here, I have affected to have
these opinions – to see what it was like –

Most Australian painting

was boring – *I* knew that: I was bored
by it! – Modernism:

I figured that was what was happening:
what we were doing seemed to come out of what had gone before

logically enough.  If it's turned out to be post-
modern, then a 'rupture', a shift of episteme

passed me by.  The way it felt I guess
when Mannerism

became Baroque: Ludovico went down to the
coffee shop – & ordered up;

Annibale entered & said,
'What's new?'

Said Ludovico, 'You tell me.'

                    *

**(Postmodernism)**

So much for my experience of it.
I love it as a theory.

                    *

What else was I talking about – notionally –
(a word of Martin's I love)

Our Notional Identity?

bad poetry?  It gets written everywhere, I guess.
I've written some myself!

I regret mine – but it doesn't amount to
grand fraud like this other stuff –

(pious hope!)

*though which is best ignored –*
otherwise, I become agitated.

I feel I should say something totalizing about
Theory


though one can't of course (step out of it /
look down from above).

But Theory is obviously the context
in which this occurs.    'I am no theorist'

is true, & yet I'm unwilling to acknowledge
an ascendancy of theory over what I do

or recognize a divide  – or a privilege, given,
to theory over poetry.

On the other hand, 'let it pass'.
I read it, of course.  Poetry must make its own.

Theory
has no monopoly on theory.


Many, maybe most, who flock to poetry
pastiche the past

in their effort to evade the future.  Very
modern of them  (or

'perennially contemporary')  I am
maybe more truly of the past

in placing any bets on poetry
for the future –

but 'it helps me feel modern!' –
the way, for a theorist, presumably, theory does.

                                                 Tho finally

this, this lecture, is mere gesture:
offering genre as an example of

'the materiality of one's practice' is rather
coarse-grained. *Why a lecture,*

even an ironic one,
if poetry is so flexible?

Perverse I guess.

– A modern, or a post-modern,
perversitousness?

                   *

And why these
'untimely meditations'?

Why *now?*
                Because

when I look back
I see these 'events' – that were

publicly on the agenda
but not on mine.

These I can date.
But what was *I* talking of –

at the time?  Were these thoughts *resolved*
& did I move on, think

something else, develop?
It seems I can't see myself

only what I was rejecting
Is it some failure, some

defeat, that they have prevailed?
But we don't expect

to easily see
our selves.

'Tiresomely one is
some sort of realist, it turns out, like everyone else' –

what else is there to talk about
but what is real – tho without,

in my case, either trying to put
my finger thru it ('take this chair,

take this table') or spin
some abstract notion about it?

Epistemology,
my nutty friend!  I have always imagined

you my goal, tho I have written often, maybe –
in moments of relaxation from your rigour –

the poem as 'consolation'
(terrible thought), the poem

as entertainment.  Ah well.
A look – untrained – at

how we know, a kind
of analytical wondering

Have I wondered 15 years
& never found out (20, actually)?

Then what was I wondering?

I seem to have wondered – almost as
set pieces – what was a fitting subject for poetry;

what can you say about
contemporary life – that is not too conclusive

total, an assertion of system; and
– as a proposition –

something as useful as
*Aren't people wonderful* ('curious',

'odd', 'interesting', 'nice')?   &
a hoping my friends

are alright.  And returned
again & again.

I have mostly despaired

at not having the brain
to put this together – unlike Meaghan – to think forward to
               something

or have, alternatively, not believed
that such were possible – & complained at the efforts of others

(The cavilling, querulous poetry
of the postmodern – or relativistic
clearsightedness?)

In the late mid 70s David Antin's
was the usage of the term postmodern

that I first encountered – I could see
what it described: but since it seemed to stem
               straightforwardly

from Modernism
I could see no sense of break – it was modernity's

selfcriticism merely.  ('A shift of episteme
passed me by.')  His explanation

had nothing tacked-on –
of the failure of the Encyclopedists' program,

of the Enlightenment, & shifts
in the world's economy.

(The 'hyperreal'
was not present.)


One catches up

with one's time –
& finds the past unrecognizable

& the future pretty certain, though
undoubtedly packed with surprises –

& a little out of time
in one's marching.

## *Untimely Meditations:* *notes & asides*

title page  The Adorno quote is from *Negative Dialectics*, but I quote it from Martin Jay's book *Force Fields*: 'I have never felt comfortable with the school's reticence about exploring its own origins, an attitude best expressed in Theodor Adorno's remark that 'a stroke of undeserved luck ...' [etc].'

'Thanks for the sour persimmons etc' comes from Daffy Duck and is spoken with his heavy lisp & withering sarcasm.

p 48  '(Each is an embarrassment)' – Tranter was a distant eminence grise – in the seventies – somewhere across the waters, who has since come home to roost.

p 49  the guy named after the biscuit – Reg Anzac? – for services to aviation? he drove a taxi? invented a biscuit?

p 50

> 'You see, I think, the / parallel with Les'
>
> The insistence on
> a locus of values
>
> represented by its picturing
> & a constituency – of volk,
>
> silent, but he
> speaks for them
>
> not Junkers, not leech-gatherers –
> Australians.

p 52  'here even, in Adelaide!'  Perhaps this is a sarcasm – has this debate surfaced, at this late date, anywhere else?  Even here it is a minor outbreak.

p 53  'the too American / too French' – Between generations & within them this might be seen as a battle of one international influence against another: Lowell, Sexton & Berryman were ok (& assimilable) but NY School

were not, nor the Beats; there were Projectivists, worhshippers at the flame
of Merwin or Duncan; there was interest in Bataille, Celan, Handke,
Schmidt …

p 53 'Australian to be dumb': it is a usual tactic of the 'internationalists'
anywhere to make a dumb/sophisticated binary here. I mean 'dumb' in
that one had (to pretend) not to know about an art from elsewhere. This
seems dumb to me, not that the 'local' method/style need itself be.

p 54 *'Tunes For Gumleaf & Fireside'* – how could I say such a thing: there *is*
no CD though Les would undoubtedly know the tune well enough and in
fact I misspelled it *Perfideo* through most drafts of this poem – so what
would I know?

p 68 'incommensurable' – incommensurable – the theoretical sublime?

p 69 Of course there are Australian artists I like – but who? A list would go
on & on and a list is not the point. My boredom was as a student: I thought,
Am I part of this Grand Narrative? I hope not. Some Wakelins, de Maistre
occasionally, Tuckson, the Ramsay portraits, some Rees, Micky Allan, Tim
Johnson, Davila, Tillers, Linda & Paul, and Kerin, Dick Watkins, the big yuks
of Linda Marrinon, Adrian Feint's 40s paintings of beach house/harbourside
suburbs, Noel's 'Everyone Must Get Stones'. The list goes on.

p 70 Ludovico: 'You tell me.' And Annibale answered, in that celebrated
phrase, 'The Baroque, of course – it's back at the house. I'll show you after
lunch.' To quote from Vasari's curiously anachronistic account of the
Carracci studio.

p 71

> I feel I should say something totalizing about
> Theory.
>
> On the other hand, 'let it pass', it is as
> much institutionalized
> as poetry –
>
> more so probably (at least they get paid) –
> & smug in its self-assurance

Which should signal complicity
with an agenda, ongoing, somewhere.  *

(*Maybe one they haven't theorized yet.)

Though why
should I hint, here, darkly?

I read it of course.
What you don't know

will hurt somebody else / bore
somebody else.

# DAZED

## The History of Nostalgia

The wish being father to the thought and mother
to your eager gestures – or at least the ones
a dulled sensibility remembers belonging to – you
stare off into the distance as hard as you can
as if some long desired form might materialise,
announcing just by its presence an end to change
& replacing this ridiculous static blur with
a perspective that creates a point of view –
something that slowly expands as you grow older,
broadening out like a real view does when you climb
a spur or wedge your way up a chimney: something
in short that doesn't tell you everything at once,
exhausting all its effects in a coup de théatre
that explodes like a trick golf ball you address
to cane down the fairway.  Instead it disappears
in a bright flash & a puff of smoke at your feet
so that you're left thinking, 'Can this be it?'
&, sure enough, it is – you're here, that's all,
another miserable subject, composed of a few jokes
& catchphrases worn smooth with repetition
but at the same time almost statuesque, like a bust
of yourself in marble or bronze & mounted on
that plinth you used to lounge against, back
when you were still smoking Marlboros & worried
you'd come to resemble your father, not yourself.

*John Forbes*

## Dazed

*for John Forbes*

The wish being
father to the thought

and mother
to your eager gestures

(that is, <u>just</u> <u>as</u> the wish is like that:
you express the wish, and *then*

– and as it is expelled
in the form of a sigh, or

huff of resignation

and maybe as the mouth, resigned,
broadens and tightens – you're an idiot,

nothing ever can be done about *anything* –

like the most welcome stranger,
who should appear at the door, on cue,

the flyscreen door of your mind, but the thought –
which both is and speaks these words:

**'Why not do it?'**

– as rejoinder
to the negativity expressed above

so that the weather
of one's mental life

– of *this* one's –
flickers

from light to dark, constantly,
like time-frame film

which looks moody
experienced as film

but as mental life
is ʻtrying'.  And thence

a whole series of gestures
is begun, as whole series often are –

remember, here, my
mental ʻlife' – and,

because of ʻthe flickering',

though begun
are cut short entirely).  You stare off into the distance

as hard as you can.  Is this
genuinely  a gesture?

one of opening out
onto new possibilities, of action?

or the will
to take a dive,

a practised motion
of your dulled sensibility,

converting 'here we go'
to 'here we go again' ?

as, characteristically, you slump,
falling from the low marble bench –

where you were viewing this vista
– Ah, this vista! –

neither mournful, nor ritzy,
but expansive and rather calming –

at any rate, where there are avenues
for claiming sudden spiritual nourishment, on the one hand,

or taking a bucolic and
melancholy reading –

of the light,
as it bounces, sharply,

off the city's buildings,
and the deepened, afternoon green of the parklands.

As if you were Poussin
or Claude Lorraine –

not Raoul Dufy.
Not *Balthus* at anyrate

– or late Derain,
that would be *very* bracing –

or late Vlaminck.
Better, probably,

not to have your
emotional life French –

better to have it Italian,

like say,
all the senators and soldiers

of a late
de Chirico

pissed out of their minds,
on speed,

milling about and carousing,
listening  to Roy and HG

with a bit of fairground music
in the background (the

kind of thing
that indicates madness,

or a bad trip,

in the poems
of Steven Kelen),

or the 'delightful' music
of Nino Rota.

In fact
from where you sit now,

looking out across the parklands,

is that little guy
planting flags at various intervals

perhaps Daniel Buren?
May be?

But though Adelaide
has embraced
much bad art

it has not, as yet,
embraced Daniel Buren.

And this is the sort of smug,
snide, superior amusement

that signifies
a wish to be

above the problem
and out of it

and which – characteristically –
leaves you
*here,*

slumped by your chair,
where you have fallen, remember?

looking
at a view,

that wastes your time,

since that is
how you use it,

through the stone pillars
of the balustrade

– since you refuse to regain your chair –
and glimpse a golfer

or some civic employee, vivid,
and tiny in the distance, place a flag.

'Get up, ya big Palooka!'
a corner of the brain urges

with your usual sense
of humour

causing another part to be smiling

– this is a
metaphorical brain:

am I like it, or is it like me?
We smile a lot at any rate –

often at the same time.
Often similarly.

Sometimes I think
I *am* my brain.

More than I am
my toe.

I look at my toe.
It is me if my brain says so.

(I always know
what it is doing.)

But it provides
stability
for the smiling madcap duo.

If something
would appear
in the park

– nothing you can imagine –

and make
some difference!

One looks for it
with longing

and no expectation –

one strikes this attitude
as a sign to oneself

of one's deserving
such an edifying salvation,

an epiphany
in green,

that turned one's soul
into a Mark Rothko painting

or the soldier – standing,
so mysteriously – in *The Tempest* by Giorgione.

What is he *doing?*

But anyway
he is doing it

with confidence,

and the sky and light
ordain that he is right to be there,

would be mad
to move in fact.

Is it going to rain?
I mean here, in Adelaide?

– It is never going to rain
in *The Tempest*. –

With a terrific
sob

your life could be over,
and you could *be* a painting.

Much of a life?

You could meet
other people,
in other paintings –

the cardplayers
in Cezanne's painting for instance –

one hundred years
waiting to make a move.

What is their cardgame,
did he tell them even?

'Hi!
What game are you playing?'

'*Qui êtes-vous?*'
'I'm a deep, grape-coloured lozenge –

normally on a sea-green ground.'
'*From a Rothko painting?*'  (Heavy French accent.)

'Yes!'
'*I guessed it.*'

One merely says,
by kneeling here,

leaning against this seat –
says a little more histrionically than formerly,
when one was sitting –

that one
deserves a rewarding vision,

a sudden, saving
sense of purpose –

that need only be an *attitude* –

in fact an attitude
would be perfect,

as who can avidly require a life of
Action, mapped out before one,

if one has come
to all this picturesqueness
merely  to sit?

If *that*
is one's idea of a good time
hell would be a life of action.

No, let others seek purpose
on the squash court.

                    One swoons
against the fake stone balustrade –

it *seems* fake,
or is it only this part,
here,

that has been replaced,

after having been
vandalized? –

to state that one is
noble enough … for such reward,
a kind of spiritual certification.

Not in the expectation
of getting it.

The *attitude*
is its own reward.

The occasions
when all stands still and
things fall into place

would be no fun if they
were commonplace.

– Life is a blur. –
One can almost feel

one is slowing events,
to bring them
sharply into focus –

like the child-care giver
who stares narrow-eyed

at the playground's
ongoing *Guernica*

in the hope his
shrewd face

will stop the perpetrator
among his charges

inflicting torment on
the rest,

despite an inability
to make out, or hear,
what is actually happening,

or to whom.  To
stroll out there

is to become part of events
– inevitably
one will select

the wrong one

or treat the culprit
too harshly

and the wheel of life
will continue to turn

and it is all too catastrophic!
At any rate, look at this mess!

Who can clean this kitchen?
You go up on the roof,

for once in your life,
to fix the roof.

It is beautiful

but saddening –
it all looks different.

The neighbour
who is mowing his lawn

wouldn't do it if he knew.
He looks silly.  The woman
putting the washing out –

silly too.

The surfers you can
see from here don't look silly.
They float on their boards –

in a sense they are
up on the roof too.

Life does not make sense.

You are standing in the wrong place.
Get down off that roof immediately.

But never forget
what it was like.

Gee –
I am about halfway
through this poem,

that I
paraphrase,

and I don't know *what* this means!
Right.  I've got a handle on it now.

It is *not* like
a trick golfball,
that explodes when you hit it.

*It is like the view!*
Or, no, it is *not* like the view.

The view
is what you wanted.

Life, though,
is not like that –
it passes us by,

while we stare,
fooling ourselves, gaining
some solace, false solace …

[John, this reads like
Tennyson!  Is it
*The Lotus-Eaters* you intended?]

You stand there,
your spirit does,
weaving about

(while your body sits,
or leans *still*
probably,

intrigued by this idea)
like an old trainer,

going  *Fsst,*
*Fsst!   Fsst-fsst!*

gloves up,
head down,

shadow-boxing.

'I coulda been a contender!'
The hopeless Nelson Algren-ness of it –
I can't bear it!

The look of disappointment
so ingrained
it substitutes for character.

You can die quietly now –

people *respect* your secret sorrow –
at the bus stop,
at the coffee shop,

the bank, the
supermarket,
thoughtfully reading the paper –

an old codger.

The reason why we like those surfers –
this is a thought –

is that
watching them

we have an ideal image
of deep daydreaming

that seems spiritual
and, in a touching way,
full of wellbeing –

the floatation tank
idea of life – an image

of our own subjectivity
while we stare at them.

And it is
'touching'

because they are
'little' –

far away – and their
aspirations

(which we can't guess
but can only suppose) –

seem fragile.

(In a sense we feel sorry
for ourselves
– via an objective correlative.)

'Pardon me,
monsieur.'

It is
the greenkeeper guy.
He bends over

and looks into
the face of one.

'Qu'est que vous?'
you say.  (Your French
is rotten.

Mine is.)

He says,
'Monsieur –
you have fallen down?'

'No,
I'm sitting,' you say,

though plainly you look
what would pass for
*completely out of it,*

sitting beside
a stone bench,

one arm stretched,
proprietorially,

lovingly,
over it.

'Are you Daniel Buren?'

'No sir.  But my
golfball – did it not pass
this way?  Did it not
hit you perhaps?'

'No, mate,
I'm just sitting here
wondering how to
seize the day.'

'It will be
dark soon,'

says the Buren figure
quietly.

A nice guy.
You rise.

# (Early Days)

*for my nieces – Angela, Tess and Michaela*

Dear Tess, to whom I wrote
last week – from here –
& Angie & Michaela, in
ten, or fifteen or thirty years
I expect you will sit,
as I do, in your regular coffee shop,
looking out on things –
with pleasure – in the noise, & scene,
though as women you may like it differently (?)
or will it be much the same.  (I imagine
your faces older – late 20s, *30s* even
for you Micky, who might grow to look like Helen Mirren
in your middle years.  Which would be interesting.
Your face – the youngest – suggests
       greater age.
Angela and Tess are closer to their early beauty.
Maybe one shouldn't wish on you,
as possibly rather glamorous types
the sort of mollusc, aeolian mental life
which I've habituated myself to.

                I put off
writing the kind of poem
I am usually happy enough with
– of rather disconnected ideas & incidental detail,
from my surrounds – either because I don't want
to 'set off' in that direction, or none of
the individual ideas seems *interesting* enough,
for me to find myself started.

                    And
now the ideas have mushroomed & chased each other
& I have a field of them, none very singular
in itself, & no way to begin.
                              In thirty years
I will be an old man.  If not a dead one.
                                        I think:
will things have changed, much, by then?  Current
wisdom would have it that Yes, the planet
will be scorched & economic dominance of the world
will be in Asia or wherever – or that No,
the patriarchy will be grinding on, the sexes will be
as individuated & effectively & badly socialized
as now.  Not that there isn't a certain rough charm
available – in things as they are.  Hardly compensation.
'The charity of the hard moments'
is a phrase that comes to mind
– an obscure reference even now.
Obscurer by your time.
                    I hope, though, you *are*
happy.  I hope you're happy in the *coffee* shop
every now & then – & think of me.
I think of you, all of you, as younger than me
– in this particular future – which would mean
that if you were here now I would be
the at best mildly interesting, but probably merely
unprepossessing, old bugger (black jeans, black T-shirt –
V-neck, unbuttoned) writing, looking out the window, looking
sort of happy, sort of mild – for an hour.
And you would be unapproachable.

        The things

I had thought & didn't write down

        – Of course,
I would be unapproachable too. –

     are these:

A cartoon I was looking at, the other night,
had a cat & dog in bed together, the cat saying furiously
'I am *not* trying to be Aloof – I'm a Godamned Cat, Okay?!'
The dog is comforting himself with a book entitled
*Dogs Who Love Too Much.*
         I taught the words to Cath's little girl of *'Men
Smart! But, the Women is Smarter'* – she only knew
the rap version – of which they've taken out
most of the words. If that's progress I guess
things won't be much changed in your day.

I'm having coffee & a peach nectar – not my usual
combination. It is hot today. I've just finished reading
Philip Larkin's letters – an English poet. By the time
you're forty his complete letters will have come out, if
there's sufficient interest in him. A very nice guy, probably –
he spent much of his life trying to be old before his time
&, vis a vis the modern world, an irrelevance. He wasn't prepared
for England in decline, though he hymned it, with a churlish
regret most find loveable, gladder to see it in him than
themselves. Certainly he made me feel young (by
contrast).
         I'm going to work now – that is, where I'm
employed – a part-time job. Some books I designed
will soon come out. It's 1993 – & as yet 'early days'.

## Paris to Pam Brown

I have hardly seen the Eiffel tower –

                            even

from a distance

             living a week in Paris

With another week to go

                I think I will

hardly see it

             I walk our street in

the Bastille

             & sit & have coffee   or a

Ricard or pastis

             or walk hours in

the Louvre

             attending   to the confident

stylish

        look of the French

                    their little

dogs

       their cars, their motor scooters,

                        zipping –

always zipping

             up on the footpaths

                       the cars

effortfully manoeuvering

                around one another –

where they have parked at an angle

               across a corner

across a drive
                        the large doleful phlegmatic man
& his timid little dog
                        (The dog stands under him
tiny & leonine, trembling
                        between the ornate curlicue
legs
        of the chair that support's *cet homme*
                                        while
a larger dog passes
                        & a small Citroen   or Opel
attempts to park
                or attempts to leave
                                a sip of coffee
& the car is gone & another one replaces it
                                I guess it *was* going
or we'd be looking at the same car, right?
                                – in the rue vielle du
temple
        where I don't see any temple, either
                                tho I see
*'something'* large & impressive.
                                I think the temples
– read, I think, synagogues – in this former Jewish
Quarter
        were pulled down
                                Slightly warmer coloured
& a Moroccan in a burnous
                        & just one
striped awning   (orange & white)
                                it would look
Eastern enough

                    – like a Prud'hon or Gerard or other
orientalist painting
                         or one of those watercolours Australian
artists did
         of the Middle East
                              while employed by the
army
         to Record Our Exploits – late Streeton or
Roberts   or whoever else went  (Dundas?)
                                   the walls
of the buildings slope back slightly in some of the alleys
& in one this slope
                    is matched by an equivalent
lean
         from the other side   out over the alley
                                        to meet
the shrinking, retreating wall opposite.
                                   It looks
expressionist, or stagey
                         those Australian paintings
were mostly empty
                    as I recall
                              or empty*ish*
                                             as
tho our tour of duty
                    was rather boring or alien
or the artist got there first
                         or too late,  after
the soldiers had moved on
                         I wonder what Paris
thinks of Pam
         – which scans so much better than

Pam thinks of Paris
                              but I wonder what she did think?
Paris thinks nothing of us
                              as I sit here sipping

or it thinks I sit badly
                              or my suit is an odd cut
Tho it's glamorous enough
                              or so *I* think
                                                  The Swiss poet
was lovely
                  & loveable partly for the dagginess of his Swiss
appearance
                  apparent to us
                                    – so apparent to Paris?
I know nothing
                  including, it appears, not necessarily even
what 'scan' means
                  (I meant only 'sounds')
                                                  I wonder
what Pam did think.
                        I don't mean as a question –
as a report on myself:  that is what I do,
                                          I wonder.
Would *she* be as beautiful in Australia?
(of a young woman cycling by)
                                          How small *are*
they, these apartments, in which these dogs & people live?

Is that black guy happier here than he would be
in London?
                  (it seems so)   How old is that, that bit

of building there

                        sticking out from behind that modern one
a pale ochre with tiles that are funny & deep red &
unusually spikey & stickle-backed?

                             & isn't the gilding a
little extreme on that figure of *Mercury*

                                   off in the distance
atop his enormous pedestal?

                       Gee, Guido Reni
is a little overrated

               & Simon Vouet definitely

                                          &

I wouldn't leave Paris  (for ages)  if I had the money

## Florence to Lorraine Lee

Dear Lorraine,
                Cath & I have made it
to Florence
                where, in part of it, I sit in
my undies
                (red)
                                at the 'bureau'  (blond)
& write to you.
                Cath sleeps
                                just
behind me
                looking comically
                                                like that
painting
                by Vuillard
                                that is chiefly grey
I think
                in which a few dark lines
                                                (black)
indicate a bed, in profile, small head at
one end
                & a peak rising at the other
where the feet might go
                                only this is
in brilliant white
                & looks like this

you will see

from this   her head

(beautiful, rested, a warm
colour)

is the opposite end

from the Vuillard
picture

My life is different to his.

Pisa

was beautiful.

If I could be a painter
& there was any point in repeating, totally,

the
emotions of the past, I would paint that sweep
of buildings facing onto the river – from a spot
on the bridge over it

looking right.

(This
places the railway station somewhere at my back
a few blocks away

on the same side of the river

as I stand
                    – for your reference.
                                        And it is
late afternoon.)
                        The water is a deep
spinach colour   that somehow has in it
                                        much else
& the grand placid sweep of the buildings
is the Italian confidence
                            that they do it right


– what? –
                build things, design, live.
They too,
            the buildings,
                            are almost indistinguishable
from each other –
                    flat facades, the same
                                        three
windows at each height
                        the buildings all as tall
as each other
                & abutted, exactly.  And their
colours
            are lovely –
                            chiefly, a range of mustard
yellows,
            some ochres, some greys, a blue-grey, a
rose, a pallid, almost-white or two,
                                    some mauves,
but chiefly those ochrous yellows
                            ranging from

jaundiced
             to a rich pumpkin-orange confidence,

the pillars or pilasters around the windows
                                                      in
dulled white & greys & bone
                                    & in the windows: shadow –
melancholy, sad, or private …
                             merely sleepy, or
inexpressive
             except to say, This is how it goes.

And overall the picture would say
                                          Calm,
                                                   an
emphatic
             but understated
                                 feast
                                          of – I don't know –
'disclosure', 'beauty', 'just proportion'


                                 Paris beauty
is so much
             more nervous, & fine-lined –
                                                   the
surface of French buildings
                                 more articulated, the
beauty more lightly & shiftingly present
                                                   the
difference between
                      Bonnard & Boldini

(If I have got the name right

                               – is he the Italian

who did society portraits

                          – family groups etcetera –

in London

               18th century?

                        a kind of bland-

ness

     that is direct –

                     conservative–understatedly

forthright.

             I am pushing it here – all these

art references –

               who will get them?     Will you?

'Sweetie Pie?'

             Cath says.   'Would you

open the window?'

               & I do.  A lovely park

is just outside

               & fills the window with

green green leaves

                 the trees of the square below.

We are 3 stories up

               & look down on a square

– the noise of birds, wind

                in the leaves, motor scooters

& distant cries

              & now a bell.    It rings for me

& rings for you, here.

\*

Well the poem ends there. I think I meant Batoni for the painter (Goldoni & whoever are probably musicians). I meant to write you a letter – but I had nothing to say so I thought I'd write a poem & 'see what was in there'. Mostly clichés.

Some guy should send photos of Cath & others from her conference. Could you send them on?

I'll write properly from Australia. Meanwhile, thank you for the stay in Paris.

Here we're in the *Andrea* hotel, whose owner we met at the railway station – cheap, very nice, & on a square –across which we look to the Duomo, which is just 2 blocks away. We've drunk already at both *Il Patriarcho* (The Patriarch) & the *Genius Bar*. Both okay.

# Perugia to John Forbes

Dear John,
                 I thought it would be nice
to send you a postcard
                      – after all,
I've had them from you while you were o/seas –

the postcard, I imagine, says
                          '& get on with the
really serious business
                    of being an Australian' –
after discussing Europe, the Louvre, the French
the British, the Italians,
                   expressing
my appreciation,
              enthusiasm even,
                      while trying
to accommodate your stated position on these matters –
that it is
          all a theme park
                  whose
virtue & annoying failing
                is to resemble itself
rather too unfailingly.
                 Tho I have never
been able to really credit this, as you keep
returning:
         People always say,
                marvellingly,

John's in Rome again – imagine!
or 'in Paris,' 'in
London'
        & one smiles imagining your T-shirted,
Newtown futurism there, a riposte to it.


(But I haven't written that card.)

*


        I *did* like it.
The Louvre
I loved
      & Paris generally was pretty nice
(I mean,
one felt light
      & pleasantly *transitory*
before the endless weight of the buildings on the
boulevards
      – finally one could see
'where the money
went'
when French history spoke
        of the cruel & crueller
& yet more cruel taxes
        the Louies levied.
It all went here:
      central government,
outrageous privilege.
      I liked the Chardins, the
Watteaus

         (& much else – but is this what you want to
hear?!)
        & was interested in how bad Reni was
with the bit between his teeth – i.e.,
                        lots of
commissions – & occasionally 'how good' – &
how bad some of the French second stringers
                  (Le  Sueur, Vouet).
& on the 'street' … the French were okay –
                 & we met
some nice ones
       (some *very* nice).
                But how
could one go & live there
           without spending a year
or more
      working thru these pointless
generalizations?
       & where you *had*, who would
you talk to –

       in the sense of
            'writing poetry to /
for'?
      what would happen to your language –
wouldn't it 'lose touch', get
           'out of' touch?
          in fact?
(So I think better to come back & get on
with the really hard work
        of … etc.)

I've seen Harry Mathews twice.

                              The only
other literary part of the trip

                              – its rationale
the thing that made it financially possible –
was Cath's attendance at the French *Poetry in
Translation* conference

                    where she, & various
poets who spoke French & English –

                                   a Swiss,
a Guadalupian, a Quebecois, an American
an Irish, a Scots & various French –
discussed the intricacies & otherwise of each
other's translations (of each other's work).
Pretty intense.

                         Harry (who is
interesting,

              & rich

                    – & entertaining as well)

                                        told me
among other things

                    that Joe Brainard was dead
had died just a few weeks back.

                              ((He also said
Why don't *Scripsi* send him copies

                              of that stuff
of his they published – as well as money, tho
as I said …))

                         I don't know if you cared
all that much

              about Joe Brainard,

                              but for me

he was part of the zep

                I associated

                            with Berrigan &

Padgett

           (& the others – Warsh, Tom Clark, early

Anne Waldman, Elmslie, Dick Gallup)

                             work

I loved & that I

                'took on board'

                          – & modified –

but

        'took on board', to say the *least*.

                          I always

think of him as young.

                (The photos – that

showed him skinny,

                with a grin & an Afro, in

jeans & jacket.)

                *I Remember*, as Mathews

                        said,

was   something to have left behind.

                      (I'd even

started doing one myself a few months back

occasionally adding to it.)

                  (Laurie's

*Adventures In Paradise* grew out of a similar attempt

on the *I Remember* model.

                Did you know that?)


                  His graphic work,

too,

      was really good.

                              I guess he was too nice
to make it in the art world (?)
                              can that be
the explanation?
                    Denis Gallagher once sent him
a postcard
              claiming fan status
                              & got a reply.


                    *


We've just been walking round Perugia
                              waiting
'for the cool change to come'
                              – as the Weather Girl on
TV said it would
                    said it so rapidly she
                              *'had'*
to be a weather girl
                    We should've guessed
                              Tho
she was otherwise bimboish
                              to a degree we don't
associate (in Australia)
                    with 'hard' information –
                                        &
we called in on the church
                    of San Philipo Neri –
beaten, but stand-up Baroque, on the outside,
& inside pretty impressive.
                    A mass was
underway, so we didn't tarry.  Earlier

we called in on one ancient ruin

                                    inside whose

grand, archaic doorway (columns,

                                    capitals etc)

                                                        was

a church the size of a small lounge-room

                                    with

real, assorted lounge chairs

                                    & a congregation

of 4 old women.  (Wow.)

                                    In San Marco

in Florence

                    there was lots of singing

                                                        a concert

so I went back to see it with maybe more lights
on.

            It was only ok:

                                    & had to restrain myself –

despite the tourism & tourists

                                    some silly old stooge

an expression of long-suffering

                                    & disdain

was waiting to give confessions

                                    you kneeled in

front of him & you & he hid, under a bit

                                    of shared cloth –

very 'in camera' –

                    I wanted

to misunderstand, try to make him sell me
… a bus ticket, a cigarette lighter … .

Siena tho was great – beautiful Siena,

                                sometimes

known

           (in Swineburne's celebrated phrase)

                                      as

'Siena the terrific'

             where, during the promenade,

on the *campo*,

               when you stare directly up,

after a bottle of wine, & a *pastis*, a *Ricard*,

a *cynar*, *un radic* or whatever

                          (not all

of these, as it spoils the view, & in fact

you land on your head

                 – tho where better,

when there are so many people

                  to help you up?) –

you see this:

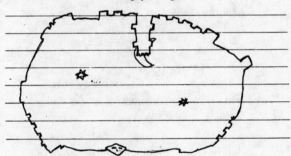

a fish's-eye view    of the sky,

                         blue,

                              buildings

all around

           (in *their* characteristic colour).

(See, a European experience, an epiphany!

                                        resembling, tho,
a football hooligan's.

                           But I thought, even so,
I should tell you.)

                       I've thought of you a lot
over here – & Pam & Laurie –

                                my
euro-travelled friends,

                    thru whom the world
has been so far filtered

                (or 'mediated')
as well as thru, say, Berrigan, Padgett (the
*'American Express'*) & Schuyler.

                         *And*
Robert Culp & Bill Cosby (*I Spy*)

                         & Roger
Moore (*The Saint*)

                 – no Henry James in sight.


TV is next door.

                Something American –
you can tell by the sparse, sparse dialogue.
What do Italians make

                    of these movies they
dub & watch, in which, unlike them, the
people are so monosyllabic, constrained,
so grim,

               where an Italian would be
emoting, gesturing at least,

                     insolently
or desperately

making meaning –

                         thru

shoulders, head, eyebrows ?
It must seem like comic strips to them.


\*


Hmm


\*


'How you gonna

                   keep him
down on the farm,'

       you said to Cath when she
rang,

    'now that he's seen Paree?'

                   This
is to let you know

         I'll be back at the
pit face

      light, transitory, but really
real

    in the hard New World, new Italian
suit to help me.



P.S.  Hi, too, to Dipti – and remember, send Harry copies.

# Poem (Up Late)

'I am always walking out on a terrace,'
– Tony Towle, *Starry Night*

'… in town and working on my poems
at Joan's studio for a new book by Grove Press
which they will probably not print
but it is good to be several floors up in the dead of night
wondering whether you are any good or not'
– Frank O'Hara, *Adieu To Norman, Bonjour*
*To Joan & Jean-Paul*

    Up,
& working on
my manuscript,
for a new book
by A & R,
which they probably won't print …
        Actually
I am reading *Locus Solus*, the magazine,
not fooling with a manuscript –
though *Adieu To Norman,*
*Bonjour To Joan & Jean-Paul'*
*is* in its pages –
& has
one of my favourite
'up at night' scenes in poetry –
O'Hara in a
white shirt,
a few flights
up, standing, looking

at something, an
ashtray,
or some art deco junk,
    holding a drink,
        reading his poems maybe.
           (A light at
           the desk,
           silence.)
       Not only
will A & R not
publish this, *where
is the romance?*
They're not Grove.
They publish mainly
shit.
      *I* am, typically,
in the kitchen – Who's to say
O'Hara wasn't? –
feeling, at least,
pleasant enough.
      'Typically',
as used here, reminds me
of Tony Towle
– from whom I've
borrowed it or picked it up.  He
is always turning to a balcony, a
window, & looking out.
Which is how I imagine him.
And who *isn't*
either – sightfully –
forgetting oneself or,
sightlessly, forgetting everything else –

the mind,
like a bladder, breathing in
breathing out – to make
a comparison
at least grammatically resembling
one of Tony Towle's?

Now who would publish that?
Thinks: *Wakefield* might.

Perhaps my oeuvre in
large part represents
a slur on the poetry of my betters –
whose example
allows me to go wandering off,
by the reeds, ankle deep
in mud,
mumbling inconsequently –
somehow 'licensed' by them,
by their example –
though heedless of it?

A mysterious traduction,
*because*, I am
often struck,
on reading them, how
familiar their words are:
'to be idiomatic
in a vacuum!',
'Excitement prone
Kenneth Koch',
etcetera.

                    One
could see this as tragic.
But I will see it that way
in another poem –
called *'Ruminations In An Emergency'* –
I won't dwell on it here.


                    What *is* my subject?


*Locus Solus* was a
terrific magazine.


I am up-late, reading it.
Schuyler, Ashbery, O'Hara –
Harry Mathews – *The Conversions!* –
Edwin Denby.


                    John rang tonight – a
painting of him, as Zeus, by Ken Searle –
with a request
to review an artist friend of his –
her request, not John's.  When
I think of my*self* –
as I always do – I think
of others:  a letter
from Laurie, a parcel - sent -
to Johnny J, recently,
a letter I owe
to Pam Brown.  And
staring sightlessly,
when I do,
from here,

I see the mobile Cath made,
of sea shells,
that hangs above
the new baby
of Max & Deb,
a photo of him,
surrounded by vegetables,
small &
intent.
                    The shells
hang creamily, above,
suspended
on string, their
fan shapes,
their casual number
reminiscent - for me -
of 50s/60s
Australian decor –
beach houses, boomerang-
shaped ashtrays,
'blonde' wood, burnt browns, bush reds,
mustard yellows, tan colours, a particular
beer-can design
from that era -
*Toohey's Pilsener*? –
of yellow
with a touch of purple
& ears, or sheafs,
of grain on either side.
Anyway, I have forgotten it.
Cath bought Yuri
some terrific pants

this Xmas
that revive that era.

       To the left of the baby
is a cartoon-figure bear
or cat
      *Hanna*
*barbera*-style
in wax, with a
wick coming out on top,
making it
a candle (though
who would light it?) & between
it & the photo, a
lemon.
      These are all
half visible,  half silhouetted,
on the half wall
that divides the
TV/dining area (where I sit)
from the serving
& cooking
area, which has its own
indirect half-lighting.
There is
lots I can see: brick, shelved
plates & cups, olive oil,
the modern stove, the
shells – nearer, Gabe's homework
amongst which I work.

# An Empty Space For Us

*for Becky Davis leaving 'her place of employ'*


*'Glad To Be Unhappy'* is the name
Of a jazz tune I like, but not as much as I
Like the title itself.  It describes, for me, a state
      of luscious
Despond.  I am not sure I ever experienced it – though
      I feel I have – 'phantom-limb' style.

When I think of it I think I think of the music on a particular
      Eric Dolphy
Album.  With that track on it. - How circular.
That is not how I felt when I heard you were leaving: you told
      me, standing
Close by, at the traffic lights on Morphett Street – I
Had to stand apart.  Must I continue to grow up, cast
      securities aside, be tough?  Why, why must you go?

For a while I could not look at you
Or speak.  'What will happen to me?'  is how I felt.
      I might even have said it –
Really, as a joke to you – but to tell you how I felt:
      sad, I tell you.  The tune is *'2  4  5'* I think:
      *'Glad To Be Unhappy'* – I don't know how it sounds.

You should play it one day.  I should tape it for you.
Oh god.  Well, I admire you & think you're terrific
      – & like you immensely.  You're off to the
Unknown.  Where I could never tread.  But I salute you

– a corny attitude my heart strikes – like the
earthlings, looking into the sky, when the superior beings
return to their galaxy, of whom they say, wonderingly, 'Will they
ever come back?' Would that you would – 'there is room
in the room *I* room in' (joke). Room everywhere.

# I'll Be Seeing You (Would That I Would Be, Too)

*for Louise Haselton, leaving, too, her 'place of employ'*

All the usual places – at the bar, at the races –
Basically, when someone your build sits
Yacking to Julie, comes behind the desk,
She'll remind me of you, and flashes – a clear memory of
Say, the way you walk across the gallery –
Intent on getting another show up and
Not doing your nut or getting panicked –
In that calm unbouncing way of yours
And your rather dry but limitless patience
with fellow workers – me mainly –

'In these things did we trust!'
Not that I always realized, till

After, your generosity.  Let's face it: I depended on it.  And, again,
('Let's face it'), you were great to bounce ideas off, test an opinion,
*Lend* me an opinion, in fact.  So often yours were better than mine – and

Even where we differed your views would temper those I had.
Though you made no effort to affect my taste in music – I guess figuring
          *What the heck?*  Though, just think, you
          Could've skipped twelve months, stranded – with me, Junior
          Wells, Magic Sam, Irma Thomas, downtown Chicago, circa 1958,
          'live' at *The Dew Drop Inn*, *The Alice Club* …

Endings are so unlike what our experience of each other
          has been - continuity, repetition.  Both

Things I like.  Some people have been
            drags to work with.  Not you.
Ciao.  Go now, conquer the hearts of Melbourne.


## II


And just as I don't really know the lyrics of
The song – *I'll Be Seeing You* – not

That it's in any way especially dumb (the Billie
Holiday *live* version, for example, is terrific) I like
            my joke version
Enough to have never remembered its

Better original – similarly, because I am dumb, or
Anyway too polite to pry effectively, you're leaving
            & I don't know you
Really as much as I might've.

After some time I realized we had a similar interest in
            class –
Not typical of the art world I think.  Yet I only know
Definitely you grew up in the country

And, though I suppose many people do,
This for me lends you an aura of 'trajectory'
            a Life Story –

That of country girl comes to the city, learns
Her way around, & moves on.  I doubt you view
      yourself as heroic, as
Even, really, the *subject* of anything approaching narrative –

Rather, like the rest of us, you see stages,
All contingent – upon luck, opportunity,
Competition.  This is becoming gloomy – dark clouds
      that are the backdrop we must
Each stand illumined against.  Seeing you that way seeks to
      Share what is real.  Like Watteau, but more contemporary, like
      Kiefer, but no big deal, (Oh, really?) – hey, like Robert Greene
      but with our clothes on!  That one wants to share it – is due to
      some talent you have.  Louise, who'd have thought it, this
      perspective, working together, behind a desk?  Well, *Cheers from
      us!* we say to you, louchely (me, Richard, Julie).

# August 6th

aeolian heart

granite granules

the film star


something  fantastic,  a


theoretical 'thing'


– from  John Jenkins

&

Ken Bolton, *The Coffee of Kings*


something
I didn't read at school.
I watched Randolf Scott movies but, on television,
and their simple morals are like the meat.  'Relative.'

Plus the song, (*Brokenhearted*), is a factor.

Mysterious money.
Those are my feelings.

a rubber brick. To
throw at people. A little *like* a brick – but jokier.


Granite granules, in the stone of the wall, catch the light –
more from the sun than the fire – the light of each
is different, as is the heat. So you can tell.


Maybe he's a comedian. – In
any case he burns now, in the fire. A 'theoretical' thing – an
article /
             on the disappearance of dinosaurs,
                               something that involves
headings – with words like 'Cambrian' –
goes up next, and other pages curl. Part of an anatomy,


of the Feeling, 'bushwhacked', I am working on. Though
I also 'must fix that fence' – something I never will.


  I say 'One false moof & I
die you,' to the kid – coming at me, unsteadily, dripping houmus
from rolled bread. He smiles.
And continues – not dangerous.


I'm
sort of famished – & sort of not – 'halfway not'
– permanent & casual my interest. But 'Ask not
                            for whom the bell tolls


it tolls for dinner'    & I eat some.

My Considered Opinion, for Michael O'Leary.


I hate to write in blue

                                   yet here I am
blue pants    blue jumper  brown table
blue pen


          buy milk, papers.


                    Anzac Day
1996

          I'm glad they didn't let

                            the Japanese

      win
Entirely the wrong frame of mind

                        they were in

back then


(&)  I'm thankful for the holiday


                        I note
the funny name

of Orlando Mourning

A magazine article
                              on childhood acquaintances
                                              of
                              the King's


– Elvis Presley –


                    had  Mary Jo Nutt


                                              (The
American journalistic classes,
                                      the
dudder academics,
                    seem to favour   all the

middle names, & initials)

                    I prefer the names
of the blues singers


                              to
                    James 'M' Krauthammer


                    An attempt
by *every*body   to sound like a President?


                                      on a

memorial medallion – John _F_ Kennedy ?

'Fox Mulder,'
                              the guy on _The X Files_
introduces himself
                              in the mumbly
                                        uninflected
voice
              I found hilarious,  for 3 weeks,
a year back



                                        Now I like best
the way
              they make Scully
                              _Agent_ Scully
run everywhere


                              hurrying here
hurrying there
                    best
                              the year she got pregnant



they put her in big coats
                              & made her    do the running
thing

like a small to medium fridge

                           a big coat with shoulder pads

totter, totter, totter

                  a letter

           to mum,

                        a letter

to  Cassie Lewis

           poet

               play

                        various

dumb  jazz &  R n B tapes

                dumb?   I mean, Am *I*

dumb?

        Not if they work

                then I am great like

they am –

        Pharoah Sanders,   Billy

                  Red

                    Love,

John Littlejohn's

        *Chicago Blues Stars*

                hang out the

washing,     fix my bike

that way lies gladness


A trial
                    to those I love,
                                        not good for the country
not part of the national reconcilliation,
                                                up
to no good


                Happy again,   with that off my chest


Ready to ask
                Can I be of use? – tho hypothetically.


'A loose cannon in his heart.'


                                        Third person ?!


Hullo, stranger!
                        Je est un autre.
                                                        *Piss*
*on the flag*
                is my attitude.        Well, actually, no –


but I like the phrase:
                        sort of American:   Lou Reed
Bukowski, Burroughs.
                        Piss on Howard.

The movies aren't on.

                              Nothing 'Anzac'.


A network decision –

                                              ...




                I knew a woman

                                        whose Dad shot
the commanding officer
                              – to the relief of the men
whom he led, then, back to safety.


Dad.
                    the one political thing he said


which he said to the TV

                                    not to me:
he leaned forward in his chair     & said
                                              'You
big urger'
                    – to Menzies.


                              I'd never heard the phrase


I guess the Menzies' push for conscription
though he'd avoided it himself

                                        the pig iron to Japan

        his continued, patronizing self-satisfaction

                                                        Confidence

        in his   'Powers of Persuasion'.




sometimes I think every night I
                would like to sleep
with you
                & then other nights
                there I am   slightly
curled
                & feeling  the way eyelids do

                in Frank's poems

slightly blue,
                fragile, stroked
                        woops! he's

astral travelling again.   **X**  says
                she is unhappy – perhaps you
should never sleep
                with anyone twice?  My heart (the Eyelid)
says,
        The only way to continue in my fragility

                    is as an

eyelid


          – arms & lung & *shoulders*
                    is the alternative –
you there  with me  or
                against me  or partly on me:
this way you will
                    live forever


                I like all the things
that alter your state *mildly* –
          a cigarette,  coffee …

                                    for these I live.



Today I bought the B.B. King tickets.


We go to sleep early
both exhausted


and around 11.30
the phone rings
                    – right by my ear –
Hazel gets it
                – it's her house –
                            and soon after

we fuck.

*

I can't sleep.

*


                    Hours after I have
stopped reading them
                    I am still thinking,
feeling rather bleak
                    – my life after all:
consider it –

            …



The rice
            Millie cooked for her boyfriend.


                    Not so bad.


                    I go to my room
around four.  Read a few more
                    Schuyler poems.



            I am
                    burning through the night    alone
(towards) – 'Bed at 5.'

when
         a gnat lands in my wine
Reminding me


                    of another hero


   I don't know.   'We
                    walk in time, our dazzling bodies
have steps ineffable'
   Mine will carry me soon
to the *Exeter*
   I am so unhappy!


                         That is a joke
   (About unhappy.)


Jokes
   *'can be <u>so</u> true'*,
                    can't they?


   'Ineffably' they will carry me


      The thing
with Frank O'Hara  – the gnat, the wine –
                 what
*did* he mean, really?  that is the tragic part:
I love those poems


146

My brain
  has failed *so many* tests
   I should not expect
much of it.

then Braque speaks
 & he seems foreign too
Lost, all of them

I shall go to the Exeter
  & explain this


Hello Pam.
   Why do I always like
the cornily romantic
R 'n' B
of the past

that leaves space
for the shameless
or beautiful voice
of the lead singer –
to go for broke

do you know that?

I've been listening to Billy 'Red' Love.

It is ages since I have
written to you.
I have been writing
art criticism instead.
And other things, but that a lot.

The new
Peter Schjeldahl is in.  I love his
reviews – my mind
operates better
                when I'm
reading him.

Why do I have so little to say?
Not just to you – I mean
to anyone?  In poetry?

Hilary McPhee can get fucked.
I met Helen Demidenko in Brisbane –
why doesn't she go & get fucked?

Could Luke Slattery really be a nice guy?
As opposed to 'intelligent bullshit-maker'?

Intelligent?  Why doesn't *he?*
I mean, what stands between us

& the deluge, but Errol Simper, huh?

Joke.

Actually I'm pretty happy

tho turning, obviously, bitter.  However

'There's no used
a me tryin' / to act so gay'
              (Billy 'Red' Love)

But I will.  There *is* a 'used'
                        (pronounced with a
                                'T')!


Billie
'Red' Love
is on now: 'Blues is an achin'
old hard disease.'
              But, no, that
is not what he said.  I anticipated.
Maybe
      he really will sing it,  somewhere in this song?

(Schjeldahl tells the story –
A father explains about
Death –

to daughter, who asks where,
having died,
the dead animal *is* –

…

   *Well,* he says, carefully,
His *body's* on the floor of his box.


Wide-eyed the little girl shouts
***WHERE IS HIS* HEAD*?!***
(Runs to dead gerbil.)


I'm putting mine 'to bed',
           *my* head.



   'Fox,'


         humbly trusting his interlocutor


     not to ask
       'What, not *Squirrel?*'


In Manet's great painting
*The Insomniacs*
the three readers
share the bed
a girl and her mother,
the other, a man, has books, too,

on the bedspread before him,

but writes in a pad – *in* pencil *on* a pad –
their story.


(*'Vuillardy'*)


  The watch hand
goes to my head, which is bent, writing, writing this.
I tell the girls, and we all look up: Anna smiles,
Cath looks 'poised' and I, because I've been concentrating,
have a frown disappearing.

Hi.


      Another Day



      outside *The Flash*.  Nope,
proprietor says
No *Guardian*
Nope, no *Age Review* (he rang &
checked


        But I know this.  (We
regularly have this conversation.)
Today
I ask him about the *New York Review of
Books*.  Nope.

        He suggests *Imprints*

across the street.  No,
        they don't get it –
*yet.* They are thinking of it maybe.


       So far
I have spent nothing,
       in fact I have been re-
funded seven dollars & 20 cents.


       No yoghurt
in the *Star Grocery* either.


Michael Zerman, *he say*    'Another day,
       another dolor.'


'The sun is shining /
on both sides of the street'

       (old song)

'Hullo Caron,
       hullo Francesca!'


later, reader, *much* later:

If only the sun were shining tonight –
or if the actress –
(who had 'killer pins')
– wherever she walked was followed by those words
a pulsating of little lights, a chorus –
it would be bright *then,*

              <u>or</u>,     '(It)
            *wouldn't be dark but,'*
(André Breton)

                  A penalizing phone call
penalizes my ear –
        with its 'ring'

                'If only my train could enter
that tunnel,'  isn't that a bit obvious,  Monsieur Breton?

Angie Dickinson, huh, in, *The Killers*?
Did you know she had 'killer pins'?  Have you in fact
*seen* the scene
where her little legs walk …
   Springtime would be terrifying then,

             *Actually* – August – it will be terrifying
any minute!

the marvellous living letters
of breasts, their imperious, pleading  'glances' –

*Cadillac Walk*

by Mink De Ville,

        all the records of whom, André, you have, I imagine,
     or you could borrow them,
   from Allen Ginsberg,

             & inevitably
                     have your photo taken
 next to him –

       thus to be remembered, your course crossing his
       in your search for love.


The sun is set; the swallows are asleep;
     bats flit past in the ash-grey air;
Vespas arrive, as from nowhere, sound,
     are gone, the noise bubbling after them.  A breath
of wind fans across the Arno's sheen
     not rippling it appreciably – the merest shiver

Aint that nice, *here we are in Pisa!*  the electric lights, the reflected
     moon.  The bridge's stone,
dry; the buildings, dry too – the wind is dry, intermitting, light.
     Need some moisturiser!  In the inconstant motion of the breeze

dust and papers shift, settle, shift again, but that's just Pisa,
          shift continuously, about

the pavements of the town, unwitnessed beneath
          the lamps, or in the dark reaches of the streets.  (In the 'deeps'
of them.)  Where the sound
          of the Vespas 'disappears' (actually 'diminishes' – *the Vespas*
disappeared though, & *I* would disappear
          after them.  But how?  On foot?  And I do not speak Italian.)


The image of the city lies along the surface of the river –
          communing with itself, placid, sad, shivering
slightly.  Not even dry, like the rest of us.  It speaks to me
          – *more clearly* than to a local – though it says much less.  (The
language problem.)  It says, *Go* –

*You will change, I will stay the same.*  The sun has sunk now
          totally.  It is as if the river sighed, became
that degree more sad, the pale ash cloud has darkened,
          the sky above a deepening blue.  I wonder
did Shelley breathe this breath, feel similarly
          the river's non-committal bearing him upon its surface.


Did he see the scene

                              where her little legs

     walk down the hall?


155

(Claire's?  Mary's?)

                                    "Should pleasure,

    in the form of a perpetually

        perambulating woman,"  lead you on, this might be

            *just the thing*,  the wick of a bomb,


                        a bomb in Pisa.


what a funny day you've been, August 6th

# Bad Memory
## (an account of a year's shows at the EAF)

*'I wonder how the year began?'*
– Dean Brown

To find out how the year began I lope
To the filing cabinets – my brain is
Shot, memory shot thru with holes.  What hope
Is there?  Even simple questions such as these –
*What day is it?  Who's prime minister?* float
Over my head.  My brain: rather like Swiss Cheese –
In the 'hole' respect.  *Before she eloped,*
Now think, *tell us, your mother's maiden name was …?*

Etcetera.  Terrible!  Did the year
Begin badly, or well?  The tug I give near

Pulls the grey filing cabinet's heavy drawer
Out, onto my foot, in fact the whole shebang
Almost buries me.  Yike!  I wrestle drawer
And cabinet back – *and. save. my. life.* Phew!  And when
I find the first show I think, Bonzer!
Remembering the general verdict then,
When **Various Small Fires** opened & collared
The attention of the local arties.  Dang

Me if'n it didn't.  Each artist was paired
With an Artist's Book – 'from the archive'.  There'd

*1*

157

Been competition, I bet, for Ed Ruscha –
Whose name rhymes with *touché* (a fact stuck
In my brain since I first read it one day
In a poem by Tom Clark) – as it happened, that nut
Steve Wigg got Ruscha, and did a palm tree, Ruscha
Style – well, a Ruscha *tree* Steve Wigg-style. 'Nut'    2
Is probably not the right word, or way,
To describe Steve, I guess. *In one word but?*

What way is a better way!  Other nutters
In the show were Thom – we all agree 'nutter'

Is the word for him? – he papered his car
In newspaper text.  That was great.  He drove
It in and parked it in the gallery.  Other far-
Out pieces were Louise Haselton's; a mauve
And ugly looking fish, of Jenni's – with a jar
Of little pellets to feed it from … Blowed
If I know whether it liked them.  He was Star
Of the show – representing the kind of cove

We don't get in art now (ha, ha) – the isolated    3
Elitist, sans audience.  Has film created

A cynical renegade from art in Jenni?    4
Art is so bad, true, I sometimes feel like the rat
Who goes and presses the button, dutifully,
Every time: and what – *nothing!*  In my rat's
Tray, sadly, no reward.  Oh well, Thom duly
Drove his car out and – 'Must I eat my hat'

158

As they say? – an even greater show: Brony,
The more *au courant* of the Platten girls, prac-

## 5

Tically blew our minds away: hotdiggety!
What a hard, yet absorbing, assemblage.  Me,


I felt my inner brow beetle, & beetle
Again, and a sense as of a desert wind
Riffling across that mental sand, little
By little, ridges raising – corresponding
To Doubt – then smoothing them, little here, little
There – their form so fitted as to *rescind*

Doubt, but yet leave puzzlement: why were these so
Curiously right? what were they so right *about?*  'Foe


Of tedium', yet scornful of the easy,
The gallery was full of disembodied
Tongues – clumsy, thick, silent – that could as easy
Name the meanings of the work (though they tried)
As we could: their inarticulacy
Mocked our own peculiar inability

To explain *why* it was good.  (I liked it.
Did others like it?)  A critical hit


With reviewers – who also seemed to love
Susan Fereday's show, **Object A** – which seemed,
I thought, obvious – well made, sure – above

All, resembling 'art', like a school project beamed
Somehow into now from the late 60s: doz-
Ens of handbags, with those ascriptions – esteemed

'Witty' (well, they were), 'double-edged' (well, true
Of some) – sort of pat.  The next show – or 'shoe'


As Ed Sullivan used to pronounce it,
Was Joyce Hinterding's.  Hmm.  For no other
Reason than her curious name I would repeat
the Take-a-letter joke, of Groucho's, with the Hunger-
Dunger name – used for the partners of a law firm – it
Goes like this (& gets repeated) *'Hungerdunger,*

*Hungerdunger, Hungerdunger & Hungerdunger!*
*Dear sirs, I draw to your attention ...'*  A bunger


Explodes in the street, say.  And *Yike!* you respond –
Which resembles the jump & shudder many gave
When Hinterding's electric whizz bang 'time bomb'
Began to tremble, quiver, machinate
So furiously, with the evil aplomb
Of a Vincent Price movie.  Whirr, ziggle, grate!

It seemed the purpose was to simulate,
Make palpable, our *wrong* & inadequate


Ideas of electricity's functioning
(As an excuse to enliven our senses –

Hearing, & sense of interval & space) – to wring
From us enriched acoustic judgements:
'Pure' installation effects, depending
On the doubtful alibi of putting dents

In archaic notions. To me, it seemed sim-
Ulations like these 'revive' ideas that rest, in-


Ert, in figures of speech (currents 'flow', are 'full'). Ghost
Trains, I was reminded of, Coney Island
Effects, looking 'gallery rigorous'. Most
Seemed to like it. I scratched my head. **Mien**
(Cruickshank) & **Faraway** (Geoff Weary) we host-
Ed next – impressive in their effects, and

Yet mute, really, as proposals. Here art
Was pleased, again, to resemble Art – art


In its aspect as auratic - is that the word? –
As having enigmatic or ambivalent
Aesthetic presence – while we shoulder the load
Of its import for it – & *it* is ascendent,
Superior to us – okay if we incurred
A dilemma that was interesting, & spent

Our lives with, somehow, ordinarily –
Like Warhol's *Disaster* series – or tragically

Grieving *Jackie*, the *Race Riots* – because  – gulp! –          *8*
Such news, & our response, are ours to live with  –
Salutary that art has us face them.  The bulk
Of **Short Sharp Shock**, which followed, were you to quizz
Me on it (which is why I'm at the files, whose bulk
Near killed me, but which I stand with now, as with


A friend, an *old* friend – we have seen a lot),
If you asked me, I'd have to say I've forgott-



En it entirely: **Short Sharp Shock**, **Short Sharp Shock** …
No, most of it is only vaguely registered.                    *9*
Andy's for example was like a sketch, though *not*
Of a thing that would be a 'Good Idea' – except
As it appeared in Andy P's brain.  Who would want
That on television?  Who wants to get


In Andy's head?  Well, **Short Sharp Shock** allowed
That pleasure – minus drugs.  As clouds suggest more clouds,



& then a storm, Andy's sketch for a TV show
Similarly suggested TV.  'I liked
The suggestion' – is that okay?  A Japano-                     *10*
Australian series – yes, I know what you might
Mean.  Ceallaigh's film, Mehmet's piece – which, to go
Past, made one tentative: so tense, yet like


Something beautiful because natural – filed
With the rest, & forgotten (for me).  Some, young, tried

Out for the first time – so a new crowd was seen.
Adam Boyd – as a child, obviously
'Messy in the kitchen' – came to the Eaf
With those same ambitions, now gigantic. He
Spread enormous chemical pikelet mix. These
Were our next show. Scale was its virtue. Only

*The Incredible Shrinking Man* had encountered
Pancake spills this size before. These we mounted


On the walls & lay along the floor. The public
Came in, & looked, & marched out again – but they
Don't understand the good shows either. Cyborid
Feminist bad-girl punks from outerspace
Or virtual space, or inner space, came quick
Upon the heels of Adam Boyd. It was a case

Of his stuff seeming timeless but forgettable,
While **VNS Matrix** seemed inevitable


But dated, 50s sci-fi, 60s, corny
& campy. Yet many found it fun – if not
Exactly challenging – or am I wrong? (or am I
Wrong to look for challenge – is that in fact mod-
Ernist? *Should* I have found it fun? Art should be, broadly
Defined, entertaining – yet basically not

Just Entertainment. (I think.) Maybe 'Art'
Is art's best idea – where we think about *it*, Art!)

The art we got next was Derek Kreckler's –
To me both too grand (as gesture) & too spare –
Romantic Modernism again?  Yet harsh
In a way I liked.  The metaphor, as metaphor,                    *11*
I didn't like; that it was money & we walked on it,
I did.  The walls looked like the veils of Morris


Louis – but sort of bloody, like Herman Nichte.                 *12*
Hm, there's dust on this filing cabinet – maybe


From my brain?? – together with a little drink
In a plastic cup, from the last opening.  *Drink me,*           *13*
It says, & *I may kill you.  I'm the milk*
*From **Various Small Fires** – I've seen a lot of*
*Openings.  I saw them all,* it confides, *& I agree with you.*
*What,* it asks, *was the rush with the filing*


*Cabinet, earlier, a bruising research into times perdus?*
*Office-worker's harikari? Aesthetic des-*


*Pond?*  Bad memory, I said.


                              *the end*


164

This poem was written on invitation for the EAF newsletter. It doesn't reflect, necessarily, the opinions of the EAF, but provides a kind of reprise of one aspect of our activities, our gallery program. It leaves out the talks and discussions of our *Art On Tap* evenings, a co-sponsored exhibition at the Union Gallery and much else – and all the daily life of the EAF.

The order of the shows is slightly wrong – owing to the bad memory the poem speaks of: Adam Boyd preceded *Short Sharp Shock*. As well, many names in the group shows do not appear. The Thom alluded to is Thom Corcoran. Andy P is Andrew Petrusevics, Jenni is Jenni Robertson. Others partially named are Ceallaigh Norman, Mehmet Adil and Alan Cruickshank.

On the invitation to *Various Small Fires* is reproduced Ruscha's image of a glass of milk; a replica of it stood near the entrance to the show as well, a glass with white plaster in it. It has hung about the place ever since. *This* is the glass that speaks to the author at the end of the poem. Which it did  – I was there and heard it.

Julie Lawton
Administrator, EAF.

1. first show of the year, named after an Ed Ruscha book.

2. a well known early Ruscha image is the palm tree.

3. This is sarcasm.

4. Robertson is fairly exclusively a film maker.

5. Bronwyn Platten's sister is a well known realist painter.

6. part of the show was 'some casts' of whole human tongues.

8. a comparison is being made. The Warhol works never showed with us.

9. This was a series of paired exhibitions that were up only briefly – purporting to show only very current work.

10. Petrusevics showed frames of scenes for a possible Japanese TV soap.

11. Kreckler filled much of the gallery with copper  two cent coins, in large nebula-like whorls. On the walls were painted dripping 'veils' of a blood colour that resembled Morris Louis' paintings.

12. Herman Nichte, an Austrian artist, does performances, and paintings – as a kind of saleable by-product – using blood.

13. Often one finds an old glass, hiding in the shelves, or on a windowsill, abandoned from an opening months or years ago.  This one was the gimmick prop, or logo, from the first show, *an image made real*, from the cover of the Ruscha book, *Various Small Fires*.

notes

*poem (Live at Birdland)* – Birdland was a famous jazz club. Chris Burns is a Sydney poet and Cindy Sherman is an American artist – and also, apparently, a bush walk for trainee rock climbers.

*poem ('I wonder what Paul will put in this')* was written in advance of a particular exhibition as part of its catalogue. The show was *Subway* and the artists Paul Hewson, Linda Marie Walker, Jyanni Steffensen, Helen James, Trevor Moore and Jim Moss. Trevor at the time worked for the (South Australian) Department for the Arts – which, like all departments, thought of itself as 'the Department'.

*poem ('Walking down from the Star')* – The Star grocery, corner of Morphett and Hindley streets, and painted blue and white, gave Adelaide, from some angles, a homely country town aspect. It is gone at last, unfortunately. Yvonne Rainer and Ronald Bladen are American artists. As it turns out, James Schuyler is not wearing a leather jacket in the photograph that I was misremembering.

*Hot January Night* – Buster Fiddess was a 60s Australian television comedian, with a past, probably, that I can only guess at, in vaudeville and clubs. Messerschmitt, who did go mad, is known for his strained sculptural representations of (every one of the 28) emotions. The painter Vlaminck did race on pushbikes.

*Untimely Meditations* was delivered at Melbourne University's *Space Of Poetry* conference in 1993. It was begun for a projected national conference on 'National Identity and Repesentation', a conference that got stalled. The conference was to have had a visual arts emphasis.

*Poem (Up Late)* – Tony Towle and Frank O'Hara are two favourite poets. Of course Angus & Robertson don't publish 'mainly shit' – how would I know, anyway? This is an expression of feeling merely. 'Ruminations in an Emergency' is a play on 'Meditations in an Emergency', an O'Hara title and the name of one of his books. *Locus Solus*, as the poem says, *was* a terrific magazine (of the 60s), American though published in France. Others mentioned are, I think plainly, poets, poets & friends, their children, our children etc.

*Empty Space* and *I'll Be Seeing* You are acrostics and written for particular occasions. The Dolphy stuff is clear enough, I hope (though the poem is itself confused about it). The artists mentioned near the end of 'I'll Be Seing You' are sufficiently well known, except possibly Robert Greene – whose paintings, as the poem makes clear, often have little naked figures in them, 'little' & 'contemporary'.

*August 6th* is an assemblage or collage of various pieces. There are many references, but as the poem is musical they are hardly insisted upon or part of any argument: it would be good to know Frank O'Hara's poems – though my poem stands only palely beside them – and the pastiche at the end is of Shelley's 'Evening: Ponte Al Mare, Pisa', with some heavy breathing from André Breton.